IT COULDN'T JUST HAPPEN

FASCINATING FACTS ABOUT GOD'S WORLD

LAWRENCE O. RICHARDS

WORD PUBLISHING
Dallas•London•Vancouver•Melbourne

Library of Congress Cataloging-in-Publication Data
Richards, Larry, 1931–
    It Couldn't Just Happen.
    Reprint. Originally published: Fort Worth Tex.:
Sweet Pub., © 1987.
    Includes index.
    Summary: Presents Biblical and scientific evidence
that the natural world was created by God rather than
through evolution.
    1. Creation — Juvenile literature. 2. Evolution —
Religious aspects — Christianity — Controversial literature —
Juvenile literature. 3. Creationism — Juvenile
literature. [1.Creation. 2. Evolution — Religious aspects.
3. Creationism] I. Title.
BS651.R526 1989 231.7'65 89-14611
ISBN 0-8499-0715-2 (formerly ISBN 0-8344-0145-2)
ISBN 0-8499-3583-0 (Paperback)

Unless otherwise indicated Scripture quotations are from the New International Version (NIV), copyright 1978 by The International Bible Society. Used by permission of Zondervan Bible Publishers.

Consulting Editors: Dr. John N. Moore, Founding Member of Creation Research Society, and
        John N. Clayton, Author and producer of "Does God Exist?" film series.
Editor: Carol Bartley, Assistant Editor: Stephanie Terry
Cover: Davidson Design, Illustrations: Rod Moseley
Interior Design: Advertising, Graphics and Marketing, Inc., Designer: Cavan Crane

Photographs:
American Philosophical Society Library, PA: p. 27.
Animals, Animals, NY: Doug Allan, Oxford Scientific Films p. 104; Raymond A. Mendez pp. 107, 115; M. A. Chappell p. 113; Donald
        Specker p. 117; Oxford Scientific Films p. 118; E. R. Degginger p. 152.
V. Gilbert Beers, IL; pp. 173, 181, 182, 183.
Biblical Archaeological Review, D. C.: Zev Radovan p. 158.
Black Star, NY: Dan McCoy p. 40; Flip Schulke p. 98.
Bruce Coleman, NY: Pat Lanza Field p. 33; Jen and Des Bartless p. 37; Julian Baum p. 56; Keith Gunnar p. 59; M. W. F. Tweedie
        p. 73; Carl Roessler, p. 93, 117; Mark Wyville p. 94; Halle Flygare Photos p. 102; Lynn M. Stone p. 103; Laura Riley p. 108;
        Alan Blank p. 110; Derek Washington p. 120; Hans Reinhard p. 120; John Shaw p. 121; Mark Sherman p. 167.
Design Photography Inc., NY: DPI pp. 7, 24, 151, 156, 169; Richard p. 121; Dunn p. 134; R. W. Kane p. 157.
Earth Scenes, NY: E. R. Degginger p. 35; Breck Kent p. 39.
FPG International, NY: David Bartuff p. 174.
Magnum Photos, Inc., NY: Dennis Stock p. 98; Michael K. Nichols p. 115; Erich Lessing p. 163.
NASA: pp. 13, 20, 21.
National Space Science Data Center, MD: Dr. Bruce C. Murray p. 18; Dr. Larry D. Travis p. 19.
Photo Researchers, Inc., NY: Charlie Ott p. 38; SIU Science Source p. 55, 69; David Parker/Science Photo Library p. 70, 125; CNRI/
        Science Photo Library p. 71; William J. Jahoda p. 82; SPL/Science Source p. 136; NASA/Science Source p. 177.
Phototake, NY: Phototake p. 10; Dr. Ram Verma p. 77; Ray Nelson p. 137; Martin M. Rotker pp. 137, 139.
Smithsonian Institute, D. C.: Photo #83-2272 p. 44; Photo #85-690 p. 47; Photo #76-4937 p. 63; Photo #929 p. 88.
University of Miami, FL: O. Brown, R. Evans, M. Carle University of Miami Rosenstiel School of Marine and Atmospheric Science p. 28.

Printed in the United States of America

4 5 6 7 8 9 RRD 9 8

INTRODUCTION

NOW! Answers to young people's troubling questions and doubts.

Today most people in our society think that the Theory of Evolution is a fact. It is taught that way in public schools. It is written about that way in newspapers and even in college textbooks. Almost daily we're exposed to news items like these:

- New fossil casts a different light on man's ancestors (*Time*).
- World's oldest fossil bird strengthens the link between birds, dinosaurs (AP).
- Harvard professor says: Creationism is not science (UPI).

Most Christian parents, and even teachers, aren't sure how to answer the questions such items raise. Many adults have doubts and questions of their own!

The doubts are understandable. Often they grow out of a basic misunderstanding. The word "evolve" simply means to undergo change. When we write "evolution" with a small "e," it simply means that something has experienced a slow or gradual change.

The Theory of Evolution is different. It holds that (1) life began as a chance combination of nonliving chemicals, and (2) that all living things today developed from one-celled creatures which (3) over millions of years gradually changed into the fish, reptiles, birds and mammals of today's world.

We can all agree that evolution, in the sense of change, happens. But evolution is *not* proof of the Theory of Evolution.

This book examines one of the most important questions of our day. What does the evidence *really* say about the Theory of Evolution? How fascinating (and reassuring) to find that the Theory of Evolution is *not* a "fact!" The truly strong evidence is *for* creation!

Because doubts and uncertainty are often planted early in a person's life, this book is written in a way that teenagers will be able to understand.

Many features make this a special book for young people and for parents—as well as a valuable resource for churches and Christian schools.

It Couldn't Just Happen:

- explains the beliefs of those who think that our world and life itself came into existence without God.
- examines the evidence that such people claim "proves" their view.
- presents strong evidence for the creation of the universe and the creation of living creatures.
- reviews some of the evidence that the Bible, which tells us about our Creator, has a supernatural origin.
- Throughout, this book helps young people and parents develop the confidence that *It Couldn't Just Happen*—and *didn't* just happen! God does exist. He created the universe and living things. And God created human beings in his own image. We need not doubt or fear. The evidence is on our side! We can freely place our confidence in our living God.

CONTENTS

PART FOUR: HUMANITY IN GOD'S UNIVERSE

PART FIVE: THE BOOK THAT DIDN'T JUST HAPPEN

EARTH IN OUR UNIVERSE

In the beginning God created the heavens and the earth.

1 THE UNIVERSE AND ITS ORIGIN

How big is the universe? How many stars does it contain? What are some of the wonders astronomers have discovered? Everything we learn about the universe fills us with a sense of awe. But even more, all we learn produces convincing evidence that the universe must have been created!

Counting the stars

If you look up at the night sky, it seems filled with stars. At first there might seem too many to count. But if you sat down and carefully counted each star we can see, you'd reach a total of 1,029.

About 300 years ago a man named Galileo invented the first telescope. How many stars would you count if you looked at the night sky through Galileo's telescope? You would be able to see 3,310.

Today, through the use of giant telescopes and radio telescopes that "see" radio waves, we know that our sun lies in a great cluster of stars, called a galaxy. Astronomers estimate that there are 100 billion stars in our own galaxy — and that there may be 100 billion galaxies in the universe!

Long ago God told Abraham, "Look up at the heavens and count the stars — if indeed you can count them" (Genesis 15:5). God knew, although in that

day before telescopes no one else could have known, that it is impossible to number the stars in his universe!

How big is the universe?

Looking at the sky at night, we can't begin to see the end of the universe. But scientists have found ways to measure the distance to the farthest stars they can find. Distances in our universe aren't measured in miles. Distances are just too vast to measure that way.

Suppose you draw two circles, one large and one small, with their centers just nine inches apart. If each inch represents ten million miles (10,000,000), your picture will show the distance between our Earth and the sun.

Now, let's say you want to draw another circle that shows where the *nearest* star will be. How far away will you have to draw it? That circle

will be forty *miles* from the sun you drew on your paper. The nearest star, Alpha Centauri, is twenty-four thousand million miles away! That's 24,000,000,000,000 miles.

The distance to our nearest star is so great that it's hard to imagine. Suppose you started out the moment you were born and ran a mile every four minutes, without stopping. You would be 700 years old before you even reached our sun, just nine inches away on your drawing! And

If the sun (on page 8) and the Earth (above) were this far apart, where would you draw the nearest star?

you would be 182 *million* years old before you reached the nearest star!

Since it's too difficult to measure star distances in miles, scientists use a different measure, called a light year. We know that light travels at the tremendous speed of 186,000 miles each second. That means light could speed around our planet seven and one-half times *a second*. Scientists use the speed that light travels in a year (a "light year") to measure star distances. By that measure, our sun is only about eight light minutes away. That is, it takes light eight minutes to travel from the sun to Earth, compared to your running for 700 years. How long does it take light to travel to Earth from the nearest star? It takes over four years.

How far away is the *farthest* object in the universe we know about? One of the farthest is a quasar named OQ172, nearly 17,000 million light years away! A quasar is a distant starlike body that gives off immense quantities of light or radio waves.

Although quasars were not discovered until 1960 by astronomers at the Palomar Observatory near San Diego, California, the writers of the Bible described the vastness of the universe centuries earlier.

Many years ago David wrote a psalm, a song of praise to God. David had been a shepherd and had spent many nights alone under the sky gazing at the stars. There, looking up, David thought:

> The heavens declare the glory of
>   God;
>   the skies proclaim the work of
>   his hands.
> Day after day they pour forth
>   speech;
>   night after night they display
>   knowledge.
> There is no speech or language
>   where their voice is not heard.
> Their voice goes out into all the
>   earth,
>   their words to the ends of the
>   world.
>   Psalm 19:1-4

Today we know the universe is more vast than even David could have imagined.

How can we measure star distances?

As astronomers studied the light from stars, they made a discovery that at first amazed them. To study light, scientists spread it out, separating it into different colors. As light shines through a crystal, it separates into colors, just as light shining

When the light from our sun is separated into its spectrum, the lines tell us what the sun is made of.

through drops of water in the atmosphere separates into the rainbow. Each color of separated light, from purple at one end to red at the other, has its own wavelength.

When light from a particular star is separated, a series of black lines appears along the band of separated light. These black lines are like fingerprints. They tell the elements the star is made of and are different for every star.

In 1962 the light from the quasar 3C 273 was studied. The black lines had *shifted* from their usual place, toward the red end of the separated light.

Other stars were studied, and many more showed a "red shift." But what did the shift to red mean? The answer stunned the scientists. Astronomers believe that the red shift means that galaxies are traveling away from us at 100 million miles an hour!

But the red shift tells us even more. The red shift increases with an object's increasing distance from the Earth. So by studying how far the black lines in the separated light have shifted toward the red, astronomers can estimate how far away from us a star is.

You can see how if you try this experiment. Mark two dots on the surface of a balloon. Blow up the balloon, and the dots shift, moving away from each other. As the universe expands, stars too move away from each other.

By studying the red shift, astronomers have estimated just how astoundingly far away many objects in the heavens are. Astronomers have located quasars that seem to be as much as 17,000 million light years distant. Not only that, but for their light to reach us, these objects must be a hundred times brighter than a whole galaxy of stars, even though they are far smaller!

What is the significance to us of the red shift? What does it tell us about the beginning of the universe?

Did our universe have a beginning?

The discovery of the red shift changed many scientists' ideas about our universe. There have always been scientists who believe in God and other scientists who do not. Before the discovery of the red shift, many nonbelieving scientists argued that the universe had always existed. If there were no beginning, there was no need to believe in a God who created everything.

But then astronomers learned that our universe is expanding—exploding outward at tremendous speeds. They realized that an exploding universe *must* have had a beginning!

Today most scientists believe that the universe began in a fantastic explosion that they call the "Big Bang," and they think that it happened about 15 billion years ago.

But what caused the Big Bang? No scientist has an answer. One science book calls this the "ultimate mystery" and says "there is no scientific answer to what happened *before* the Big Bang." Then the writer goes on to say that "we must accept that the universe did *begin*." [1]

For Christians, this is no surprise at all. The Bible tells us that "in the beginning God created"(Genesis 1:1). We already knew that the universe was created from nothing—by our God.

Of course, we do not know *when* God created or how. The Bible does not say that creation took place as a Big Bang or that it happened 15 billion years ago. Yet we do know from the Bible that there was a time when God spoke, and everything sprang into existence. Yes, the universe did have a beginning. And only if God exists can that beginning be explained.

An orderly universe

Our universe is a cosmos, not a chaos (a confused mass or mixture). The word "cosmos" comes from the Greek word *kosmos* and means "orderly universe." It is the order of the universe that lets scientists discover and describe the natural laws that govern it. Such laws have been found to govern everything from the behavior of the atoms that make up all matter to the movements of enormous spinning galaxies. The methods of science and the very concept of science are rooted in the notion that the universe is orderly.

For instance, a scientist might observe traffic patterns in an unfamiliar city. He or she watches streams of cars stopping, starting and flowing on again. After carefully noting how individual cars and groups of cars behave, our scientist would try to understand the laws that govern vehicle behavior. For instance, he or she might suggest a Red Light law: "All vehicles, except those with flashing lights or sirens, must stop at red lights." Of course, there would be one problem. Some drivers run red lights and go through them when they aren't supposed to. But in the universe, natural objects cannot choose to violate natural laws.

Using this basic approach of observation and description, scientists have found that *all* the physical universe behaves in an orderly way, with all things following their own sets of laws.

As scientists have studied the laws that govern the universe, they have found other surprising things. For instance, if these laws were just slightly different, life could not exist. Our existence depends on a great number of precise rules that govern nature, from the behavior of atomic particles to the behavior of stars and galaxies. Only the perfect balance that exists between nuclear forces and electrical forces allows the existence of stars and planets. For example, only the precise amount of gravity on the Earth allows people and animals to walk about freely and, yet, not fly off into space. There was no margin for error in the establishment of these laws.

But where did these laws come from? There must have been starting conditions that established the laws. In fact, everything scientists have found proves that only very special and unique starting conditions could possibly allow for the development of an orderly universe. Actually, *any* starting condition marked by chaos appears to end not in order, but in more chaos, without stars, galaxies or life! So the order and structure scientists have described in stating laws like the law of gravity exist only because *that order was established within the universe at the moment of its creation!*

It is one thing to try to explain the Big Bang without God. It is another to try to explain the establishment of natural law at the moment of creation without God.

The law of entropy

One of the most important natural laws known to science is the Second Law of Thermodynamics, often called the law of entropy. This law tells us that anything which is organized

This spiral galaxy is like our own Milky Way. There are about 1,000 million stars in it.

tends, with time, to become disorganized. Originally this law was linked with the science of heat energy. But it has been found to apply to every physical process, from how atoms operate to the chemistry of our own bodies. It is because of the law of entropy that scientists believe our sun must eventually burn out. Many scientists think that entropy is the cause of aging and physical death. Because of its application to all things, Albert Einstein viewed the Second Law of Thermodynamics as the premier law of all science.

How does this important natural law apply to the question of the origin of the universe? Very simply, it tells us that our ordered universe *could not* have developed from chaos! The principle that the Second Law expresses—that everything tends toward disorder rather than order—is deeply imbedded in the nature of the universe itself.

The law of entropy then is powerful proof that the universe must have been orderly at its creation, with all natural laws in place. For our universe to exist as an ordered place today, its starting condition must have been orderly as well.

It seems obvious that only God could have built laws into the universe that make it exactly right for life. It is beyond belief that the universe came into existence in an ancient Big Bang and at that moment orderly relations in the universe were established by chance.

And yet, many scientists continue to believe the unbelievable. Why?

Why doesn't everyone believe in God?

It seems puzzling. Nearly all scientists now believe that the universe had a beginning. It seems obvious that something must have caused that beginning. The tremendous energy and power flooding our universe could hardly have just happened. The only reasonable explanation we can imagine is God. But still, there are many people who don't believe in God! Why?

Romans 1:18 says that men who do not believe "suppress the truth." That is, they simply will not believe, whatever the evidence. And there is evidence!

> What may be known about God is plain to them, because God has made it plain to them. For since the creation of the world God's invisible qualities—his eternal power and divine nature—have been clearly seen, being understood from what has been made, so that men are without excuse.
>
> Romans 1:19-20

This Bible passage helps us realize something important. Even the strongest evidence won't *make* a person believe in God. In fact, some people will make fun of Christian beliefs even when the evidence is on our side.

It's also important to realize that some scientists even argue for their theories against the evidence because they insist on trying to explain things without God.

We just saw that scientists who accept the Big Bang theory are sure that the universe must have had a beginning. In this they agree with the Bible, which also teaches that our universe had a beginning. But a few scientists still argue that the universe, not God, has existed forever.

One theory holds that the universe had no beginning and keeps on expanding forever. As galaxies move apart, new galaxies just "spring into existence" between them. This theory is very strange. Where do the galaxies that "spring into existence" come from? Astronomers have found no evidence that this theory might be true.

Another theory holds that the universe explodes outward only so far and then falls back in on itself due to gravity. It falls back toward its center, until it explodes in another Big Bang. This theory has no evidence to support it and is not a scientific theory at all. And even if such a thing could happen, the theory still must explain how the *first* Big Bang happened. So most modern scientists who study the universe do believe

Galaxies, which have millions of stars, have different shapes and forms.

that the universe had a beginning. The Big Bang is *"the accepted view."* Even so, many scientists who accept the Big Bang do not believe in God!

But just think a minute. Is it reasonable to think that something could begin without a cause; that the universe could begin without a Creator; that natural laws present from the beginning could govern our universe without their being designed? Not really. Every reasonable conclusion requires God! And *no reasonable explanation other than God has ever been offered*!

It is really not enough to say that the Big Bang "just happened." How much more reasonable it is to believe that God exists and that the universe exists because it was made by him.

More wonders

Those who study the stars constantly find new wonders. There are radio galaxies which give off the energy of a million stars, not as visible light but as radio waves. There are quasars, bodies whose super-hot discs outshine a hundred galaxies. And there are pulsars, rapidly spinning stars that have collapsed and become very dense. If our sun were to turn into a pulsar, it would shrink from being 865,000 miles wide to being just 15 miles across!

The spinning stars are called pulsars because each time the star spins it sends out a burst, or pulse, of energy. How fast do pulsars spin? Our sun spins, or rotates, about once a month (every twenty-five

days). Most pulsars spin about once every second, and we know of one pulsar that spins thirty times a second!

The more we learn about the universe, the more strange and awesome it appears. Yet everything is ordered; everything is ruled by natural laws whose only possible source is God!

An astronaut's wise word

Two Russian cosmonauts, Yuri Gagarin and Gherman Titov, returned from orbiting Earth and reported that they hadn't seen God anywhere in the heavens. How foolish. Colonel Jack Lousma, a U.S. astronaut, wrote that "even after traveling 24,400,000 miles, I really haven't gone anywhere."[2] Colonel Lousma went around the earth 858 times, and each orbit took ninety-three minutes. Yet, as he says, light travels that far in less than one-seventh of a second! How far out in space have human beings explored? Imagine dividing one second into a thousand parts. If the known universe is 15 billion light years across, human beings have traveled out into space just 1.5 thousandths of a light second!

How foolish of Gagarin and Titov to speak as if they had explored the whole universe, when they had hardly traveled away from Earth at all! How foolish to speak as if they expected to see God peeking around the moon!

As the Bible says about God, "The heavens, even the highest heaven, cannot contain you" (1 Kings 8:27).

God is not just out there among the stars. God created the stars. The universe itself is our strong evidence. We know from what God has made that he does exist.

Just For Fun

1 Take a friend outside at night and ask him to hold out a dime at arm's length. Then ask him to guess how many stars that dime covers. (The answer: 15 million!)

2 Measure off a mile and then time yourself as you run it as fast as you can. Write your time here _____. How long would it take you to run, at that speed, from Earth to the sun? (HINT: There are 1,440 minutes in a day. First figure how far you would run in a day. Multiply that number by 365—the number of days in a year. Then divide 93,000,000, the approximate number of miles to the sun, by that number.)

3 Sit outside one night for five minutes, just looking at the stars. Then read Psalm 8. Can you understand how the psalmist felt? How did you feel?

4 Astronaut Jack Lousma says that while he can see God's work in the heavens, what is most important is the effect God can have in our lives. Lousma writes, "I pray daily to God, asking him to guide me. I have seen him directing my life." Which do you think is the best evidence for God's existence: the universe or God's effect in your life? Why?

5 Look up the Big Bang in a science book or encyclopedia. What do you find?

2 DEAD PLANETS, LIVING WORLD

Nine planets ring our sun. The more we learn about the other planets, the more unusual Earth seems. Each of the other planets is a dead—and deadly—place. Only our Earth is a living world.

What is the solar system?

The solar system is made up of our sun, nine planets and their moons, and thousands of other bits of matter called asteroids and comets. Gravity holds all these things in space near our sun. The sun itself contains nearly 99.9% of all the material in its system.

Each of the nine planets swings in a great circle around the sun, traveling through space at terrific speeds. Mercury, the planet closest to the sun, travels at 110,000 miles an hour and takes just eighty-eight days to go completely around the sun. Earth is speeding through space at 67,000 miles an hour and takes 365 days to circle the sun. The farther out a planet is, the slower it moves and the longer it takes to go around the sun. Pluto, the ninth planet, is moving at only about 10,000 miles an hour and takes about 248 years to make its circle!

Each planet also rotates so that different sides face the sun. It is the rotation of our planet every 24 hours that makes night and day.

The Bible reminds us that when God made the Earth and the heavens, he said, "Let the land produce living creatures" (Genesis 1:24). The more we learn about the other planets in our solar system, the more we realize that only Earth's land could possibly provide a home for living things.

What are the other inner planets like?

The planets are often divided into two groups, the inner and outer planets. The inner planets are those closest to the sun, and they are solid rock. The inner planets are Mercury, Venus, Earth and Mars.

For many years people have wondered what it is like on our neighbor planets. One astronomer a hundred years ago thought he saw "canals" on Mars. Soon people imagined there were whole civilizations of "little green men" on the other planets. Science fiction writers wrote imaginative tales of what life might be like on Mars and on Venus.

But now the inner planets have been carefully studied by scientists. Space probes—pilotless spaceships filled with special instruments—have flown by each planet. Space probes have even landed on Mars and Venus. Today we finally know what it's like on the surface of each of these planets.

Let's imagine that we're on an expedition to each of the inner planets. What would we find if our spaceship tried to land on each in turn?

Landing on Mercury?

TOO HOT!

Excitement grows as our ship approaches Mercury. Instruments on board tell our crew that Mercury is very heavy, perhaps heavier than

This photomosaic of Mercury was constructed of 18 photos taken at forty-two-second intervals by Mariner 10. The north pole is at the top, and the equator extends from left to right about two-thirds of the way from the top. A large, circular basin, about 800 miles in diameter, is emerging from the day-night terminator at left center. Brightly rayed craters are prominent. Taken from a distance of about 130,000 miles, the pictures were computer enhanced at the Jet Propulsion laboratory.

we'd expect for its small size. Perhaps there are expensive metals to mine there.

As we come closer, we examine the surface of the planet by telescope and find that Mercury looks very much like Earth's moon. There are flat plains and craters of all sizes. And look. There's the patch astronomers call "weird terrain." Part of Mercury's surface has piles of giant jumbled-up cliffs and shattered mountains! And on the other side of the planet is a great, flat bowl—a huge crater that takes up a tenth of the planet's surface.

We realize that a giant rock from space must have struck Mercury, making a dent on one side, and so shocking the other side of the planet that its surface was literally cracked apart.

Mercury is close to the sun, and we've learned that it rotates very slowly. In fact, from sunrise to sunrise on Mercury is 176 Earth days. We'd better make one more check before we land. Mercury gets a lot of sunlight, and it looks hot. It might pay to make a temperature check.

When we do, we discover that the average noon temperature on the surface of airless Mercury is hot enough to melt lead! We'd better not land on Mercury. If our spaceship didn't melt, it would quickly become so hot that we would literally be cooked inside it!

Landing on Venus?

We're hopeful as we approach Venus. That planet is about the size of Earth, and we can see that it's covered by clouds. What is under them? Since we can't tell through a telescope, we bounce radio and radar waves off the planet's surface. When we do, we're amazed at what we discover.

Venus is rotating (spinning) *backward*, but very slowly. In fact, Venus turns only once every 243 days. Underneath its cloud cover, the surface

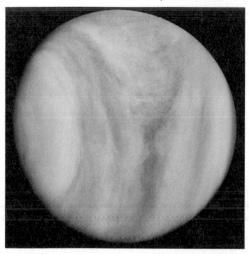

This full-disk image of Venus was taken by the Pioneer Venus Orbiter 40,000 miles from Venus. This phase angle, or the variation of illumination of Venus, has never been seen from Earth.

of the planet shows mountains and valleys. Many of the valleys are far deeper than Arizona's Grand Canyon.

But can we land on that surface? Will we find a warm, green paradise under the clouds? The answer comes from space probes sent down through the clouds. The rocks on Venus glow dull red. And its clouds trap heat under them. Even though Venus is twice as far from the sun as Mercury, Venus is hotter! The surface rocks on Venus are 870°F.

What's more, the air of Venus is very different from Earth's. Its atmosphere is deadly, made up almost entirely of carbon dioxide. And those clouds aren't water vapor, like Earth's. They seem to be made up of droplets of sulphuric acid. What's more, the clouds are lit up from within by hundreds of bolts of lightning that flash every second. No living thing that we know could possibly survive on Venus!

We turn away, realizing that we can never visit Venus, much less try to live on her. Venus, like Mercury, is a dead and hostile world.

We land on Mars!

Mars is only half of Earth's size. Yet it has valleys and mountains larger than any on Earth. Mars has no water vapor. But as we approach the planet, we can see lines that look like dried-up riverbeds. As we circle the planet, we realize there is no running water.

Our tests explain why. First, Mars is cold. Its average temperature is 40° below zero! What moisture there is on Mars is frozen. Second, the atmosphere around Mars is a hundred times thinner than Earth's. In such thin air any water on Mars would instantly boil away. Still, even though it's cold on Mars and the air is terribly thin, we can land there. And we do!

One of the scientists who worked on the *Viking* probes, which landed on Mars, has described what we find:

To get a feeling for what Mars is like, you might think of yourself being there on a camping trip, and your job is to try to make a fire and boil an egg. The first thing you discover is that there is no fuel on Mars; there's nothing on the surface of the planet that will burn because there's only a tiny trace of oxygen in the Martian atmosphere. And finally, if you chipped some

Space probe pictures show us the dry, empty surface of Mars.

water off the polar cap (there is some water ice, buried under dry ice) and put it in a little pan that was fueled by an electric heating device, you'd discover that the ice wouldn't melt into water. It would simply begin to disappear into gas, because water in liquid form can't exist on Mars. There isn't enough atmospheric pressure to allow it to remain a liquid. So that's Mars as we find it now—a dry, cold, desertlike planet with no possibility for life, as we know it, to exist there.[1]

Even though Mars is more like Earth than any other planet, we couldn't exist there!

The outer planets

What if we turn away from the smaller planets that are closer to the sun and try to explore the outer planets? What will we find there? Again, we know far more about these planets today because of space probes that have flown close to them. But nothing we find is encouraging.

Jupiter, king of the planets

Jupiter has been called the king of the planets because it is the largest planet. It is so large that it could hold over a thousand Earths inside it!

But Jupiter is not a solid planet. It is made up of compressed gas, a slushy mix of ices and vapors. Most of Jupiter is made of hydrogen and helium, the two lightest gases, compressed by Jupiter's gravity. Despite Jupiter's great size, its gravity is only 2.65 times that of Earth!

Jupiter is spinning rapidly, once every nine hours and fifty-five minutes. Its giant size and rapid spin set its atmosphere whirling violently in broad bands. Our ship could hardly pass through the greater-than-hurricane force winds, and even if it did, we'd find no solid place for our spaceship to land.

But one fascinating thing has been discovered on our flight. Like Saturn, Jupiter too has rings. But its rings are made up of dark, dust-sized rock, unseen from Earth.

Saturn, the ringed planet

Saturn is another giant planet. Yet it is less dense than water. And its gravity is only a little greater than that of Earth.

Like Jupiter, Saturn spins rapidly—once every 10 hours and 14 minutes. And it's cold, being over 800 million miles from the sun.

American space probes sent back these spectacular pictures of Saturn's rings.

Again, we clearly can't land on Saturn. But as we fly by, we're fascinated by the bright rings that band the planet. The rings of Saturn contain thousands and thousands of icy fragments that reflect light. Why does Saturn have so many bright rings? Where did all their material come from? No one has a sure answer.

Again, we know we can't land on the soupy surface of this giant planet where winds rage at 1,000 miles per hour! We have to move on, outward, farther away from the sun.

Uranus, Neptune and Pluto

WAY TOO COLD!

Uranus, just four times the size of Earth, is more dense than Jupiter or Saturn. This gas giant with a solid core rotates on its side, but backward, like Venus. Its "year" brings each pole forty-two Earth years of winter! Since Uranus' average temperature is 350° below zero, we decide not to try to land there.

Neptune is almost a twin of Uranus. The Voyager space probe will fly by this cold, distant planet in 1989.

At its closest point, Neptune is over 2.6 billion miles away from the Earth. So not very much is known about it, except that it's too cold for us! So it's on to Pluto.

The planet usually farthest from the sun is also the smallest. It is not only smaller than Earth; it is probably smaller than our moon.

Pluto appears only as a faint dot of light even to Earth's largest telescopes. It was not even discovered until 1930. A study of its surface suggests that Pluto is probably composed of frozen methane gas and weighs only one-fifth as much as our moon. Since Pluto is gripped in unbelievable cold, we decide there is no use in approaching it. And we turn our spaceship back toward home.

Dead planets

R.I.P.

On the way back to Earth, we consider what we've seen. Life exists in our solar system, but only on one planet of the nine. Each of the other planets is not only dead but sooner or later would destroy any living thing that visited it.

Actually, our voyage to the planets was unnecessary. We could tell from Earth that they are dead worlds. The law of entropy tells us they must be dead worlds. On a dead world, chemical reactions have run down. Such worlds are in equilibrium: no fresh chemical activity takes place.

The baked surface of Mercury is powdery and dry, its elements condemned to disorder. Neither Venus nor Mars could support life, for their atmospheres are "well known to be in dull, chemical equilibrium."[2] These can only be dead worlds, whose atmospheres are almost entirely without oxygen.

The outer planets offer no hope for life. They are cold, composed of light, liquified gases. We would be crushed by their deadly and ferocious atmospheres.

No, these are truly dead and deadly worlds.

The odd planet OK!

Even from space, Earth looks different from the other planets. It hangs there, bright and blue, its skies dotted with floating white clouds. It hangs in the emptiness, circled by its moon, looking warm and friendly.

Astronomers have rightly called Earth the "odd planet." In so many ways it is different from all the others. The other inner planets are pitted by craters caused by the rocks that hurtle through space. The sur-

face of Earth shows fewer signs of craters.

Moons of other planets are not nearly so close to their planet's size. Our moon is one-quarter the size of Earth itself.

Earth's atmosphere is made primarily of nitrogen and oxygen gas, with water vapor. The other planets appear pale yellow or orange or pink or red. Not one has the free oxygen that is essential for life.

What's more, only on Earth does water exist as liquid on the surface. It is water, covering two-thirds of our planet, with its vapor suspended in the air, that makes life possible here and gives our world its beautiful blue hue.

In each of these ways, and in many others, Earth is unique in the solar system. It is as if Earth were purposely hung in space, at just the right distance from the sun, and provided with just the right amount of every element needed for life to exist.

It is no wonder that astronomers who have compared what we have on Earth to everything they have found in the solar system have called Earth "*the* mystery planet." They realize that Earth is different. But they have no real explanation why, except to suggest that every condition needed for life to exist on Earth has "just happened."

Why is the sun so important? THE BOSS

Nearly all the energy used by living things on Earth comes from our sun, which is at the center of the solar system. So for us, it is by far the most important object in the sky.

Yet our sun is just one of 100 billion stars in just one of the universe's 100 billion galaxies! Most of the stars in our galaxy are either red stars, whose surface temperature ranges from about 4,000° to 6,000° F, or are blue-white stars, whose temperature is ten times hotter.

Our own star is one of the smaller and more unusual, a yellow dwarf. It is an unusually mild star, yet we can hardly imagine the awesome power it produces.

At the sun's core is a nuclear furnace, whose heat is at least 15,000,000° C. Particles of light, called photons, that carry the light and heat energy our Earth needs, are produced in the sun's core. Around the core is a wide band of slightly cooler, but still compressed and blazing hot, gas.

To picture what happens, imagine a photon rushing away from the core. On its journey it runs into atoms of gas. It bounces off, and within a fraction of an inch, runs into more atoms. Back and forth the photon bounces, moving up and down. Each time it hits and bounces, the photon loses some of its energy. Finally the photon reaches a place where great bubbles of boiling gas form and hurl up toward the sun's surface. Carried upward, the photons are finally flung out into space.

How long does it take a photon to get from the core to the boiling surface of the sun? The present estimate is that a photon must travel for 10 million years! But that long journey is extremely important to us. If the photon had not lost untold energy in its struggle to the surface, it would be a powerful ray that would destroy living things on Earth.

Even the structure of the sun

Our sun's planets differ in size, in distance from the sun, and in other important ways.

seems to be designed to bring us safe energy, warming and supporting life on Earth, rather than destroying it.

Even though photons have lost much of their energy in the journey up from the center of the sun, no life could exist on Earth if we were not also protected by an envelope of air and a magnetic field. That magnetic field repels most particles that stream toward us from outer space. As we'll see in another chapter, our atmosphere, which stretches up 18,000 miles from sea level, further protects us from the sun's rays.

How important is it for our Earth to receive *just the right amount* of energy from the sun? Even a tiny change would transform our planet. Just 1% less energy, and Earth would soon be covered with ice. Just 1% more, and Earth would soon be unbearably hot. Yet the energy Earth receives is just right—and has remained just right through all human history.

A zone of life H_2O

Earth alone in all the solar system contains a "zone of life." Only here can water remain liquid, and oxygen abounds in free, active form. While all this may seem odd to people who do not believe in God, nothing about Earth seems odd to Christians. The Bible tells us that

The earth is the Lord's, and everything in it,
  the world, and all who live in it;
for he founded it upon the seas

and established it upon the waters.

Psalm 24:1,2

Another praise psalm in the Bible also focuses on water, one of those things which makes Earth so "odd." As you read the psalm, think about

Even in this photo taken from space, Earth seems to be a friendly, welcoming planet. It is the solar system's only host to life.

the specialness of our Earth. And think about the special concern God shows for living things. For:

He set the earth on its
    foundations;
  it can never be moved.
You covered it with the deep as
    with a garment;
  the waters stood above the
    mountains.
But at your rebuke the waters fled,
  at the sound of your thunder
    they took to flight;

they flowed over the mountains,
  they went down into the valleys,
  to the place you assigned for
    them.
You set a boundary they cannot
    cross;
  never again will they cover the
    earth.

He makes springs pour water into
    the ravines;
  it flows between the mountains.
They give water to all the beasts
    of the field;
  the wild donkeys quench their
    thirst.
The birds of the air nest by the
    waters;
  they sing among the branches.
He waters the mountains from his
    upper chambers;
  the earth is satisfied by the
    fruit of his work.
He makes grass grow for the cat-
    tle, and plants for the man to
    cultivate—
  bringing forth food from the
    earth:
wine that gladdens the heart of
    man,
  oil to make his face shine,
  and bread that sustains his
    heart.

                    Psalm 104:5-15

Yes, the Earth does belong to God.
This planet is odd because God has

shaped it as a home for you and me
and for all living creatures. How important then we must be to the Lord!

Just For Fun

1 If you could travel to one of the
planets, which would you
choose? Use an encyclopedia to
read about that planet.

2 How many ways does the planet
you chose seem to differ from
Earth? How many things about
that planet make it impossible for
life to exist there?

3 Visit a planetarium or find someone with a telescope to look at
the planet you read about.

4 Write a fiction story about visit-
ing the planet of your choice. Tell
what a visit would be like and
what might happen to you and
your spaceship.

5 Do you think Earth "just happened" to be different from the
planet you chose? Why, or why
not?

3 THE "ODD PLANET"

It's not just that many features of Earth have to be just right to support life. What is most amazing is that many complex processes must continue to operate in delicate balance for our planet to continue to be a zone of life.

What if?

It's easy to imagine a few simple changes that would make life on Earth impossible or very difficult. For instance, Earth spins as it circles the sun. This gives us day and night. Earth also is tilted 23° from upright as it spins. It is the spin *and* the tilt that give us our seasons. What if Earth were not tilted? The poles would be much colder, and the equator much hotter. Without the tilt, only half as much land could be lived on, and many kinds of plants and animals would die.

Earth's spin and 23° tilt give us our 24-hour day, our four seasons, and our many different climates.

Earth is not a large planet. Yet its size is exact and essential. If it were too small, Earth's weakened gravity could not hold either our air or water. And thinner air would provide no protection from the 20,000 or so meteorites that rush toward Earth daily. With thinner air, temperatures would drop, and life could not exist.

If Earth were twice as large, the atmosphere would be pulled closer to its surface. Everything would weigh eight times as much, and that weight could crush most living things.

If Earth were twice as far from the sun, it would receive only one-fourth the amount of heat we now receive. Living things would freeze during winters twice as long as now. If Earth were half as far from the sun, its surface would get four times the heat and would become a burning desert.

If Earth did not have a large moon revolving around it, there would be no tides in the sea. Waters of the oceans might grow stagnant, unable to provide the oxygen that fish need to live.

Any of these changes would make life on Earth impossible. Our world had to be just the way it is, placed just where it is in the solar system to be in a zone of life.

Earth isn't going to lose her moon or suddenly jump closer to the sun. But it isn't just the big things which affect life on Earth. The existence of life also depends on many active processes that take place right now. For instance, what if there were no rivers in the sea?

Rivers in the sea

The Gulf Stream is one of the most famous of the rivers in the sea. Benjamin Franklin, in 1786, told of a conversation with the captain of a whaling ship. In it he learned of a current of faster waters that flows like a great river in the Atlantic

In 1786, Benjamin Franklin published a map of the Gulf Stream, one of the rivers in the sea.

Ocean. Franklin even made a chart to mark its course.

Today we know that that river, the Gulf Stream, carries 5,000 times as much water as the Mississippi and twenty-five times the water carried in all Earth's rivers combined! It is warmer and bluer than the surrounding sea, and the warmth of its swiftly moving current keeps Great Britain from having frigid, unbearable winters.

What is the Gulf Stream? Modern satellites have helped us realize that it is part of a *gyre* (pronounced *jire*).

Photos taken from satellites show some of the swirling currents caused by gyres, great rivers in the sea.

This is a wheel of moving water 13,000 miles around, circling in the Atlantic Ocean. The Pacific has a gyre, too. It touches Japan and then swings outward to bring warm waters to the coast of California. The Pacific gyre is called the Black Current because its waters are such a deep blue.

What causes these gyres? They are caused by strong, steady winds blowing from east to west on each side of our planet. It is friction from the winds and the spinning of Earth that sets the waters moving and maintains each current's flow.

Each current in the sea sets the waters below it flowing, too. Loops of water break off and form slow-moving whirlpools. Deep currents as well as the surface flow are caused by nothing more powerful than the winds, blowing steadily on the surface of the sea!

But is this important? Yes! One science book explains.

If the ocean depths were truly stagnant, as was long believed, they would fill with death and decay; for the remains of all that lives in the sea fall toward the bottom in a slow and steady rain. Without deep currents to stir things up, noxious fumes would slowly gather near the floor and kill all the bottom-dwelling creatures. Slowly the Earth's own body heat would warm this foul black water until it was hotter than the water on the surface. Then, as oceanographer Tjeered van Andel has written, "the unstable ocean would eventually turn over and vent the whole mess to the surface, with catastrophic effects on the fauna and flora [animals and plants] of the surface waters and perhaps poisoning the atmosphere.[1]

The circulation of water on our planet, with the constant motion of those rivers and currents in the sea, is one of the processes on which life on our Earth depends.

What could go wrong?

As we noted, Earth is unlikely to jump away from the sun. But what concerns some scientists are little changes in the processes that are necessary to enable Earth to support life.

In fact, what puzzles many scientists is the fact that changes in some of these processes *haven't* happened! When so many things could go wrong, thoughtful scientists have been forced to wonder, why haven't they?

The greenhouse effect?

One thing that worries some scientists is that Earth might experience a "greenhouse effect." Today there are only about 300 parts per million of carbon dioxide gas in the atmosphere. Carbon dioxide is made of one part carbon and two parts oxygen. It is the important gas that plants "breathe," using the carbon and giving off the oxygen that human beings and animals breathe. Humans and animals, in turn, breathe oxygen and exhale carbon dioxide. Carbon dioxide is also given off by burning oil and coal and wood.

Today there are more and more people on Earth, and many of the forests that used to cover our planet are being cut down. And today we burn more and more fuels. This means that the amount of carbon dioxide in the atmosphere is increasing.

The problem is that carbon dioxide gas in the atmosphere tends to keep in heat rather than to let it escape into space. With much more carbon dioxide in the atmosphere, Earth might possibly become a giant greenhouse, and Earth's temperature would rise.

Some scientists have calculated that if we keep on burning fuels and

Cutting down and burning forests to make farmland destroys plants that use carbon dioxide. Scientists worry that a buildup of extra carbon dioxide may turn Earth into a giant greenhouse and cause a global catastrophe!

keep on cutting down forests at our present rate, in fifty years the carbon dioxide in the atmosphere will double. This would drive up the temperature worldwide about three and one-half degrees.

But would just three and one-half degrees make a difference? Yes, it would make a huge difference. The greatest effect would be at the poles.

Ice at the North and South Poles would begin to melt. The Antarctic ice cap could break apart, and if it did, the oceans could suddenly rise dozens of feet! Miami, New York and other coastal cities would be drowned!

What's more, the pattern in which air flows around our world would change. The midwestern United States, where our grain is produced, would lose rainfall, and its dried soil would be blown away as dust by the winds.

But will the Earth become a greenhouse? No one is ready to say. In the past Earth has always seemed able to adjust, although no one really knows how. If a warmer Earth led to increased clouds, and they blocked out just 1% more of the sun's energy than now, that could cancel the effect of the extra carbon dioxide.

The terrible termites

The greenhouse effect danger isn't just from carbon dioxide. There are other gases in Earth's atmosphere as well. The fifth most abundant is methane gas. Methane gas too is a greenhouse-producing gas.

Where does methane come from? One source is termites, which produce methane when they digest wood.

But how could tiny termites be a danger to our planet? A scientist named Pat Zimmerman was in Guatemala to measure the gas rising from volcanoes. One day out of curiosity he put a Teflon bag around a termite nest—and watched in sur-

Tropical termites, living in mounds like these, add millions of tons of methane gas to the atmosphere each year.

prise as the bag filled with methane gas.

Zimmerman began to study termites all over the world. He found methane gas pouring out of termite mounds everywhere. And, wherever he found people cutting down Earth's tropical forest, he found termite populations exploding.

Still, how could that be a problem for the whole Earth? We realize it could be a problem when we learn that every year people cut away forest areas about the size of the state of Connecticut. In the tropics there are possibly fifteen hundred pounds of termites for every human being on Earth! Zimmerman has figured that these termites alone are adding *100 million tons* of methane gas to our atmosphere each year! And this amount increases yearly as more forests are cut down.

There are other sources of methane gas as well. But it is stunning to think that something as tiny as the termite has the potential of dangerously changing conditions on our entire planet.

Holes in the air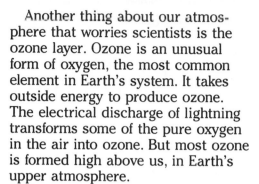

Another thing about our atmosphere that worries scientists is the ozone layer. Ozone is an unusual form of oxygen, the most common element in Earth's system. It takes outside energy to produce ozone. The electrical discharge of lightning transforms some of the pure oxygen in the air into ozone. But most ozone is formed high above us, in Earth's upper atmosphere.

There ozone is broken down by a particular wavelength of ultraviolet radiation from the sun, but is replaced as oxygen continues to produce ozone. Why is this process important? Because it is this process that removes the particular form of radiation that is deadly to life on the surface of our planet! It is the formation of ozone in the upper atmosphere, and ozone's higher concentration there, that protects life from some of our sun's most harmful rays.

What worries scientists is the discovery that the ozone layer of the atmosphere, between eighteen and twenty miles up, seems to be growing thinner. A recent discovery showed that there are actually holes in the ozone layer over Earth's poles!

Some have argued that gases in aerosol cans (spray cans of deodorants, paints, insecticides, etc.) combine with the ozone and break it

down into regular oxygen. More recently other scientists have linked the holes in the ozone layer to sunspots, great flares shot out by the sun that from Earth look like spots on its surface.

Actually, no one knows just why the ozone layer seems to be thinning. No one even knows how thick it is supposed to be! All that scientists know now is that the formation of the ozone layer is one those processes that has to operate for life to continue on our planet.

A major mystery

While ozone is a recently discovered wonder, oxygen itself is a major mystery. Oxygen is one of the most reactive of all elements. That is, it is quick to combine chemically with other elements. Two parts of oxygen combined with one of hydrogen produces water. If we mix these two gases, they do not remain separate. They quickly and actively bond to each other.

Oxygen quickly bonds to many other elements as well. Actually, about 46% of the mass of Earth's crust is oxygen, combined with metallic and nonmetallic rock!

As we saw in chapter two, on a dead world chemical reactions have stopped, as life-supporting gases have bonded with other substances. Such worlds are in equilibrium—no fresh chemical reactions are taking place. On a dead Earth, the atmosphere would be about 99% carbon dioxide. Mars and Venus are dead worlds right now. Their atmospheres are in chemical equilibrium and contain no free oxygen.

On Earth the air is 21% free oxygen. Chemical reactions that maintain just the right amount of oxygen in our atmosphere keep on taking place, and keep carbon dioxide at about .03%. For life to exist, *this balance must have been maintained from the beginning*! Without oxygen, animals could not breathe. If there were just a little more oxygen—25% instead of 21%—the whole world would actually burst into flames!

One scientist-inventor has written a book on Earth's life-supporting systems. In the book, *Gaia: A New Look at Life on Earth*, James Lovelock argues that Earth acts like a living thing itself, constantly adjusting to keep every condition right for the living things on it. Lovelock does not know *how* Earth adjusts. But he is sure it must. If the support processes were not kept in constant balance somehow, life would not exist here now. Lovelock argues that too much has gone right to credit luck, and too much that could have gone wrong hasn't. Lovelock says that there is about as much chance for this to "just happen" as there is for a blindfolded person to drive safely through rush hour traffic![2]

But Lovelock does not turn to God to explain the wonders of our living Earth, even though he has no other explanation to offer. Yet the more that Lovelock and others discover about Earth, the clearer it becomes to us that our planet was designed and did not just happen.

Everything testifies to the fact that "God made the earth and the heavens" (Genesis 2:4).

That fundamental law of nature

In the last chapter we noted that those who study our universe have discovered and described "laws" that operate in nature. One of the most fundamental is the Second Law of Thermodynamics. The Second Law, often called the law of entropy, says that any physical system left to itself will decay. Instead of being highly organized, like our Earth's systems, everything will break down. Chemical processes will reach equilibrium, that dead state found on Mars and Venus.

But the processes that operate on Earth remain highly organized. These processes are not breaking down! The atmosphere, the oceans, the relationship between plants and animals, all seem designed to take energy from the sun and *use it in an organized way*! Instead of breaking down, these processes even seem to adjust constantly to maintain that delicate and perfect balance without which all life would end.

The Russian scientist Dr. Boris P. Dotsenko was once head of the nuclear physics department in the Institute of Physics in Kiev, Russia. Although he was taught not to believe in God, he began to think about what it means for Earth to be the way it is in spite of the Second Law. Later he wrote,

As I thought about all of that, it suddenly dawned on me that there must be a very powerful *organizing* force counteracting this disorganizing tendency within nature, keeping the universe controlled and in order. This force must not be material; otherwise, it too would become disordered. I concluded that this power must be both omnipotent [all-powerful] and omniscient [all-wise and all-knowing]. There must be a God—one God—controlling everything![3]

Later, in Canada for further studies, Dr. Dotsenko found a Bible.

Reading the Bible this Russian scientist met the God who he had become sure *must* exist. Now a Christian, Boris Dotsenko has stayed in Canada and teaches physics at several schools and universities.

Not every person who studies science will reach the same conclusion as this Russian who was brought up as an atheist. But the evidence is there. Everything around us, including the delicate balance in nature that makes life on Earth possible, makes it clear. Our world didn't "just happen." Our world was designed, and even today Earth is guided and protected by God.

Living things, like our planet itself, are able to use energy in an organized way and counteract the tendency toward disorganization. This simple fact convinced one Russian physicist that there must be a God controlling everything!

Just For Fun

1 Look up one of the following cycles (balanced systems that make life on Earth possible). Look up either the water cycle, the carbon dioxide cycle or the oxygen cycle. How does the cycle suggest it was planned rather than just happened?

2 Use sheets of plastic wrap, taped to a wooden frame to make a small, *totally enclosed* greenhouse. Put one thermometer inside and another outside. Leave the greenhouse outdoors, and check the temperature on both thermometers at noon, 3:00 p.m. and 6:00 p.m. What do you discover? How do you explain temperature differences?

3 When you burn wood, oxygen in the atmosphere combines with carbon in a chemical reaction. Drop a small piece of burning wood in a jar and cover the jar tightly. What happens? Why? (As the free oxygen is used up, the reaction stops.) What would happen to Earth if free oxygen in the air were not replaced in some way? What can you find out about the processes that keep just the right amount of oxygen in our air?

4 If you had been brought up in Russia and taught that there is no God, what do you think would be most likely to bring you to believe in him?

5 If you found a radio, you would be sure that someone had made it and that it didn't "just happen." List all the reasons you can think of *why* you would think someone made the radio. How many of the same reasons make you think that God made our world?

4 WORLD IN THE MAKING

A study of planet Earth raises many questions. **Earth was not always the way it is now.** **Tremendous forces have been at work, shaping and reshaping the surface of our planet.** **We find evidence of these forces,** **but even so we know very little about Earth's past.**

One day almost thirty-four hundred years ago, in the Aegean Sea between Greece and Turkey, a forty-nine-hundred-foot mountain shook. Then it exploded with the force of hundreds of hydrogen bombs. Hot volcanic fires shot miles into the sky, causing a fiery rain that spread out for miles, dropping ash 100 feet thick on nearby islands.

Then the rest of the island of Santorini dropped into a deep hole in the sea, causing tidal waves hundreds of feet high, rushing outward at 200 miles an hour. Those waves smashed again and again into Crete, the nearby island center of a great civilization, and into other shores. Hundreds of thousands of people were killed, and the Minoan civilization was wiped out.

Many people believe that stories about Atlantis, a mythical land that supposedly sank into the sea, are really stories about the Minoans and that terrible volcanic eruption.

An exploding volcano in the Santorini Islands created a 1300-foot-deep hole in the sea and destroyed the ancient Minoan civilization.

Today we can still see the results of the eruption, marked on the surface of our Earth. We can dig through the volcanic ash that buried the nearby islands and filled the valleys of Crete, seventy miles away. We can measure the hole in the sea that the volcano blasted out thirteen hundred feet deep. And we can see the huge building stones on Crete that were torn from ancient palaces and tossed about like match sticks.

Yes, there is evidence on Earth's surface of the terrible cataclysm (a violent, sudden change or disaster) that took place over thirty-four hundred years ago.

Shaking the foundations

The explosion of Santorini was a great catastrophe. Its recent discovery is just one of many discoveries made in the last twenty years that have affected the science of geology, which deals with the study of the Earth and its past.

For decades geologists accepted a teaching called "uniformitarianism." This is the belief that what we find in Earth's rocks and on its surface can be fully explained by processes taking place now. Uniformitarian geologists rejected the idea that Earth ever experienced any great catastrophes, such as the Flood described in Genesis. They argued that natural processes could account for everything, given enough time.

Uniformitarians taught that sedimentary rocks were formed from deposits laid down by flowing streams

and local floods. At the same time wind and rain gradually wore away hills and mountains. The mountains were formed by a slow lifting up of the ground or were caused by volcanoes. All this happened in a slow, gradual way.

Today, however, discovery of events like the great Santorini blast has shaken the foundations of uniformitarian thinking. Uniformitarian geologists have been forced to accept the idea that great catastrophes have had a vital role in shaping Earth.

Disappearance of the dinosaurs

Dinosaurs are the most fascinating of fossil creatures. We do not know how long they lived, but we do know that they seem to have died out suddenly. What happened to the dinosaurs? No one knows. But most scientists now believe they died in some great catastrophe.

The name "dinosaur" means "terrible lizard." There were many different kinds of dinosaurs. Most people are surprised to learn that many dinosaurs were small, about the size of modern chickens. But some were very large.

Fossil bones of the largest known dinosaur were found near Albuquerque, New Mexico, in 1986. This dinosaur has been named Seismosaurus, which means "Earth Shaker." Earth Shaker was between 100 and 120 feet long. He stood 18 feet tall at the shoulder and 15 feet tall at the hip, and he probably weighed between 80 and 100 tons. Today a large elephant

Giant lizards once lived on Earth and then died out. Why did the dinosaurs die?

weighs only 7 1/2 tons.

Some dinosaurs lived most of their lives in water, as the hippopotamus does. We know from their teeth that these dinosaurs ate plants for food. Others, like the tyrannosaurus, were meat eaters. They fed on other dinosaurs.

The fossilized bones of many dinosaurs have been found. The soft parts of their bodies have decayed, so we can only guess about the color and organs. But there are animals alive today that are much like dinosaurs. The Komodo dragons of Indonesia, although only about twelve feet long, and the alligator, that may grow to nearly twenty feet, are be-

lieved to be living relatives of the dinosaurs. According to the *National Geographic Magazine* (October 1967), just 500 years ago a dinosaur bird about ten feet tall still lived on the island of Madagascar! Even so, it is clear that the giant lizards and most of the tiny dinosaurs are not living today.

It is not too surprising that dinosaurs aren't living today. Many species of animals have died out in the past. In the early 1800s great herds of bison roamed America. Today only a few scattered buffalo are kept alive on farms or ranches. In 1800, billions of passenger pigeons literally darkened the skies as they flew by. Passenger pigeons are gone now, and the body of the last bird to die has been stuffed and placed in the Smithsonian Institute in Washington, D.C. We've all heard of "endangered species." Many kinds of birds and animals in our day are in danger of dying out, too.

The dragon lizards of Indonesia and our own crocodiles have been called "living" dinosaurs. Looking at the pictures, can you see why?

So it is not surprising that the dinosaurs are gone. What is surprising to the uniformitarian scientist is that the dinosaurs seem to have died out *suddenly*, and their bones simply disappear from the fossil record. In some rock strata there are dinosaur bones and even dinosaur eggs, but in rocks right above them there is no evidence of dinosaurs at all.

Was Earth struck by a giant asteroid?

One increasingly popular theory was developed by a team headed by Nobel prize winner Luis Alvarez and his geologist son, Walter. They believe that an asteroid the size of Manhattan Island struck the Earth. Such a giant rock, hurtling through space, would hit our planet with terrific force.

The Alvarezes argue that the asteroid's impact would have thrown enough dust into the air to darken the skies for up to ten years. As evidence they point to a clay layer 1/2 inch thick, in which the element iridium is thirty to sixty times too high. This layer is found all over the world and seems to mark the end of what geologists call the Cretaceous period. It is possible that as much as 3/4 of all living things might have died out if such an event occurred. With the planet darkened by atmospheric dust, years of cold could have caused a catastrophe. Even months of darkness would have caused countless deaths. Perhaps the dinosaurs died out because they could not survive the changes such an asteroid would cause.

Most scientists are willing to believe that Earth was struck by asteroids. They even agree with the Alvarezes' evidence that an asteroid hit Earth off the coast of Scotland.

Many twisted dinosaur fossils suggest that some died in a terrible catastrophe.

They point to a hole there on the ocean floor 820 feet deep and 50 miles across.

But other scientists do not think an asteroid made the dinosaurs die out. There might have been the millions upon millions of tons of dust, as the Alvarezes think, yet rains would wash it from the atmosphere. The asteroid strike might have cooled the Earth for a time, but would it have darkened the planet for years? No one knows for sure.

What is important is that at last people who believe in Evolution are looking for causes beyond our planet to explain what has been called the "great dying" of the dinosaurs. For many years *any* catastrophe theory was laughed at because of science's uniformitarian bias. In fact, one famous British geologist, Dr. Derek Ager, has published a book to show that *all* the basic formations of Earth's crust demand a catastrophic explanation. The last words in his book claim that "the history of any one part of the earth, like the life of a soldier, consists of long periods of boredom and short periods of terror."[1]

This crater was made by a meteor that struck near Flagstaff, Arizona. If the Earth had been struck by a giant asteroid as the Alvarezes believe, it would have made a hole many times larger than this one.

The "death star" theory

Two University of Chicago scientists have come up with another theory. They think there have been many "great dyings" of plants and animals on Earth. What is more, they think these mass dyings have happened regularly, every twenty-six million years.

The scientists, J. John Sepkoski, Jr. and David Raup, wondered what single, regular and terrible event could cause such disaster. They think the cause might be in space.

They think that somewhere in the sky a small, dark star swings around our sun. They argue that this star comes close enough to affect the cloud of icy comets (called the Oort Cloud) that circles our sun out beyond the farthest planet. When this happens, they say, many of the comets are pulled out of their path and plunge toward the sun. On the way, some of them strike Earth. It was these icy comets, Sepkoski and Raup say, that chilled Earth and made the dinosaurs die out.

Few scientists believe the death star theory. And the death star, which Sepkoski and Raup named Nemesis, has not been found. In fact, one scientist thinks the notion of a sudden death of the dinosaurs due to an asteroid or death star is "science gone absolutely bonkers."[2]

Yet other scientists think these theories make an important point. No longer should scientists think that everything we find on Earth must be explained by what is happening on our planet now. *Something outside our planet, beyond the natural processes geologists can observe today, may be needed to explain the record in the rocks!*

Continents that move

Without question no theory has had greater impact on modern geology than the theory of continental drift. More than any other discovery, it has shaken the uniformitarian bias of geologists and led to a revolution in scientific thinking about Earth's past.

Enduring mysteries have constantly plagued the science of geology. Geologists could not explain many features of Earth. In the Sahara Desert, one of the hottest places on Earth, French geologists have found areas of deeply scratched and polished rock, as if caused by glaciers. They have also found desert sandstone swept into giant rock ripples by powerful currents of water! This sandstone, up to 100 feet thick, stretching for hundreds of miles, is a record of ancient rushing waters written in the stone.

In 1960 a party of geologists found thirty-inch-wide dinosaur tracks only 800 miles from the North Pole. Yet scientists believe dinosaurs were cold-blooded. They could not have survived in the frigid climate far above the Arctic Circle. To make things worse, the footprints led straight up the side of a towering cliff! Somehow the gigantic slab was turned on its side.

Even more stunning, the top of Mount Everest and tops of other mountain ranges contain rocks and fossils that were once under water! When was the top of the Earth's highest mountain under a sea? And how was that rock lifted over five miles above sea level?

Today because of the newly accepted theory of continental drift some mysteries may be explained. The crust of the Earth is not a single, solid sheet. Scientists have learned by studying earthquakes that Earth's outer shell is cracked, something like a giant eggshell. The center of our planet, its core, is about twenty-two hundred miles in diameter. Scientists believe that there is a solid inner core and a liquid outer core of molten iron and nickle. Above the core is the mantle, about eighteen hundred miles deep, composed of lighter but also very hot rock. The crust of the Earth—the hard layer on the surface of our planet—rests on top of the mantle. That crust is only six to eight miles thick under the ocean, but is twenty to twenty-five miles thick under continents. Under the seas, Earth's crust, which seems to be solid, is really only about as thick as a thin coat of paint would be on a house!

This crust contains huge rock islands, called *plates*. All our continents rest on one of these plates. There are about twenty plates, and they seem to drift slowly about on the surface of the Earth.

When the idea that continents drift was suggested in 1915, people laughed. The notion was argued by the German scientist, Alfred Wegener. Wegener noticed that South America "fits" against Africa, like one single piece of a jigsaw puzzle fits into another. But the scientific community ridiculed the idea. The theory seemed to call for some terrible cataclysm to explain how the continents could have moved.

In fact Wegener was not the first to think that the continents once had

Layers of sedimentary rock were formed of minerals deposited by water. Broken and twisted sedimentary rock is evidence of powerful forces that have also shaped the crust of Earth.

been together and then split apart. In 1666 a French monk wrote a book titled *The Breaking Up of the Greater and Lesser Worlds: Or, It is Shown That Before the Deluge* [the Genesis Flood], *America Was Not Separated From the Other Parts of the World.*

But in 1915 most scientists were committed to uniformitarianism, and anything that seemed even to imply a cataclysm was automatically rejected. So they laughed at Wegener's idea.

Today geologists think the continents *did* drift—and today are still

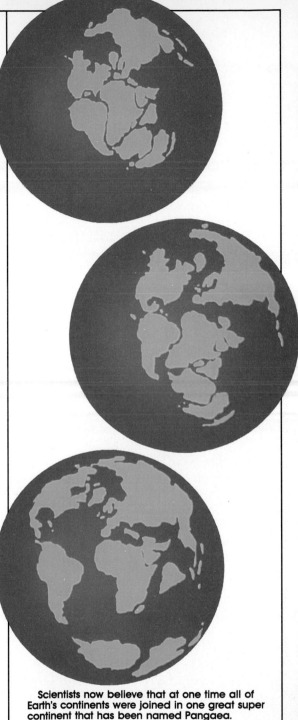

Scientists now believe that at one time all of Earth's continents were joined in one great super continent that has been named Pangaea.

moving away from each other, but at the rate of less than an inch a year! As the great plates on which the continents rest drift, superhot lava rises slowly along great undersea faults (valleys that are like deep cracks in the sea bottom). As the lava squeezes up from below, new sea bottom is formed. It is believed that even this tiny movement, and the pressures it creates, cause most of the earthquakes that disturb our planet every year.

Because scientists believe that the continents are drifting now, nearly all have come to accept the idea that once, long ago, America and Africa and Asia and the other continents were linked. Together they formed a super-continent that is called "Pangaea," a name that means "all Earth."

Today geologists explain many of the mysteries on Earth by using this theory. They say the Sahara Desert in Africa may have drifted from the South Pole to the Equator, where it lies today. The glacier that may have caused scratches in the desert's rock may once have been an ice cap at the South Pole.

But even this theory cannot explain all the mysteries discovered on the surface of our Earth, as we'll see in the next chapter.

Cataclysms on Earth?

That word cataclysm is an important one. It means a violent and sudden change, or a disaster, that affects the Earth's crust. Geologists, who once ridiculed catastrophe theories, today realize that cataclysms have happened in the past.

One writer says,

> Today, now that earth scientists have accepted Wegener's vision of shattered and sundered continents, it is easier, perhaps, to contemplate other catastrophes in the record: the sudden onset of ice ages, the nightmare notion of the runaway greenhouse, the monstrous flooding of the scablands. It is only recently that such rude shocks to the Earth have entered the domain of sober and respectable discussion in scientific journals. It is interesting how much of our thinking about the Earth is shading toward catastrophe theories.[3]

Much of Earth's history will remain forever mysterious. But one thing is clear. What scientists have recently learned about Earth's past points toward a world shaped not only by slow processes, but also by cataclysms.

What about the Genesis Flood?

There is no question that the Bible describes a terrible Flood in ancient times. That Flood undoubtedly occurred. What is uncertain is just what effect the Flood had on Earth's crust.

Some Christians believe that the Flood is the best explanation for the thrusting up of many mountain ranges and even for the initial break-up of the continents. Many creationists have pointed out that fossils have been found, jumbled together, as though swept into place by an overwhelming flood of waters. At the present, though, we can't say for sure just what features of Earth the Genesis Flood is responsible for.

What we can say is this: Today most geologists scoff at the notion of a worldwide flood just as they once scoffed at the notion of other cataclysms. Yet they can no longer deny that important features of planet Earth have been shaped by cataclysms. Perhaps soon more evidence will enable us to tell just what effects are results of the Genesis Flood.

Just For Fun

1 Look up meteors in an encyclopedia. What do you read about cataclysms that have been caused by meteors?

2 Trace the continents on a map of the world. Ask a friend to try to fit the shapes together like a jigsaw puzzle. Ask your friend to explain what he discovers.

3 In 2 Peter 3:3-7 we read about people who believe that "everything goes on as it has since the beginning of creation." Are they right or wrong? Why? What do you think this passage has to do with scientific ideas about the history of our Earth?

4 Another volcano that erupted was on the island of Krakatoa. Look it up in an encyclopedia under volcanoes or vulcanism. What happened when Krakatoa erupted? How many volcanoes are there on Earth? What kind of cataclysms might volcanoes have caused?

5 Read what the Bible says about the Flood in Genesis 7:11-12, 19-20. What features of the Earth do you think might have been caused by that terrible Flood?

5 MYSTERIES OF THE EARTH

Earth's crust contains many wonders. **While the theory of continental drift seems to explain some things that once seemed mysterious, it does not explain many other mysteries.** **Science textbook writers that speak so confidently about the age and features of our Earth often ignore the mysteries, just because they cannot be explained.**

Many features of Earth bear silent witness to a cataclysm or cataclysms that may have helped shape land surfaces, but which cannot be explained by gradual continental drift.

About sixty years ago, Russians in northern Siberia found the remains of a frozen mammoth, a giant woolly elephant that lived long ago. What shocked the world was that the mammoth had been frozen so suddenly that it was still chewing its food! In that beast's mouth, part of its last meal was preserved. It had been eating delicate grasses and flowers called buttercups!

Other mammoths were found, too, their flesh so well preserved that steaks cut from them were cooked and served to the Russian scientists and to members of the Royal Society in London, England!

How can we explain it? How did herds of fat, well-fed animals, grazing on grasses and buttercups in warm fields, suddenly freeze to death—so quickly that their last mouthful could not be swallowed and—so quickly that their fresh meat was

What happened to this mammoth, found flash-frozen in northern Siberia? Flesh on the head of this woolly creature had been eaten by wolves, but the rest of the animal was perfectly preserved. How could it, and other animals, have been frozen to death almost instantly, with the buttercups it was eating still unswallowed in its mouth?

preserved for thousands of years?

No one *can* explain it.

Did the crust of the Earth suddenly shift, sweeping these ancient beasts northward toward sudden, arctic death? No one knows. But none of the theories advanced can explain the find—or can explain the other animals such as wild horses, giant oxen and giant saber-toothed tigers that are also frozen whole in Siberia's arctic muck.

Whatever happened, it is clear that some terrible cataclysm, which affected not just the herds of animals but also the surface of the Earth, was involved.

Mountains where they shouldn't be

The theory of continental drift holds that mountains are formed when the great plates on which the continents rest drift together and collide. The tremendous pressures crack Earth's crust, piling up the surface rock to make mountain ranges.

This means that mountain ranges should be found along the *edges* of the continents. But what about mountain ranges like our central and southern Rocky Mountains? From what geologists know now, our Rocky Mountains simply shouldn't be there, any more than quick-frozen woolly mammoths should be found in Siberia.

There are many other features of North America that also do not fit. The Colorado Plateau is a great block of sedimentary rock hundreds of miles wide. That block of rock seems to have been lifted up, still lying flat rather than tilted or broken. How could that have happened? No one knows.

The Badlands in our Dakotas have been carefully studied, and geologists agree that their rock formations were formed by rushing waters. But these too are hundreds of miles wide. Where did unbelievable masses of rushing water needed to carve the Badlands come from?

Throughout the United States, geologists have located what is called "suspect terrane." This phrase is used to describe masses of land which are close together today, but which geologists believe could not have originated together. San Francisco's Golden Gate Bridge is 9,266 feet long. Yet geologists think that the land on one end must have been developed at least 1,000 miles away from the land at the other! In the San Francisco area geologists have found ten different terranes, one of which contains fossils of animal life found only in the ocean near the equator!

Some geologists have concluded that our whole continent is like a patchwork quilt, made up of bits of land that they think first formed in Asia or Africa or on various ocean floors. How could this have happened? How could the bits and pieces not only come together at the edges of our continent, but slide up on the giant plate on which North America rests and settle down on its center? Geologists have difficulty answering these questions. And yet they know that somehow it must have happened.

How old is the Earth?

One of the ways that scientists deal with mysteries is by appealing to time. They may not know just how something happened. But given billions of years, they feel that almost *anything* could have happened.

So an important question is, how old is our Earth, anyway? The date of creation and the fact of creation are two separate and distinct issues. The Bible tells us that God created the universe. The Bible teaches that God shaped Earth as a home for humankind and created the living plants and animals. The Bible does *not* tell us *when* creation took place.

God's world contains much evidence for creation. Earth, the only planet we know of that can support life, is special. As we'll see, living creatures are so unique that there is really no chance at all that life could just happen. We'll also see why the many different and complex living creatures on Earth could hardly have developed from a single, ancient cell, as evolutionists think. All this is evidence that God exists and that he is our Creator. But none of this tells us the date of creation.

Modern scientists who accept the Theory of Evolution think that Earth was formed billions of years ago. They think the animals whose fossil remains are found in Earth's rocks lived millions of years ago. And geologists have worked with other scientists to date different kinds of rocks and different fossils.

For instance, these scientists say that the Eocene period, when they once thought the first horses appeared, began 55 million years ago. They say that the Devonian period, when they think the first amphibians and freshwater fish appeared, began 400 million years ago.

Even though these scientists speak confidently about such dates, the record in the rocks is not as clear as they would like people to think. Just as scientists talk about the Theory of Evolution as though it were a fact instead of a theory, so they give dates to different rocks and fossils when it is not at all certain those dates are right!

How scientists use fossils to determine age

One record found in the rock is reasonably clear. Remains of plants and animals, called fossils, are there, and similar groups of animals usually (but not always) appear in similar strata (layers). In general the mammals are found in higher layers of rock, dinosaurs in middle layers, and water animals called trilobites in the lowest layers.

The Theory of Evolution says that over millions of years, larger and more complex animals developed from earlier, different kinds of animals. Evolutionists have decided that "trilobite rock" (the lower rock in which trilobite fossils are found) is therefore *much* older than rocks with other kinds of fossils. This "trilobite rock" is called Cambrian, and evolutionists think it is 550 million years old!

Now, it's true that where trilobite rocks (Cambrian) are found below rocks containing other fossils, the Cambrian rocks were usually deposited first. But the sequence of deposit tells us nothing about age!

For example, we know from history that George Washington and Abraham Lincoln were both presidents of

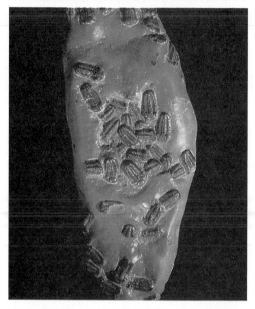

Evolutionists say that these trilobites, preserved as a fossil, lived 550 million years ago. But can we really tell how old they are?

the United States. If we knew only that Indians lived here first, and that Washington was president before Lincoln, we could only guess at *when* these things occurred.

How do we know that Lincoln was president in the 1860s and Washington was president in the 1780s and that Indians alone lived here before 1600? We know because we have a written history and a common dating system. We count time from the birth of Christ. And many written

documents that give dates tell the story of Europeans coming to America and stories of Washington and Lincoln.

But when it comes to rocks, we have no written history. There was no one who wrote down a calendar date when a particular layer of rock was deposited. We might know which rock strata came first, but that alone does not tell us *when* the rock layers were laid down. So ages given to various strata of rocks are at best an educated guess.

What is radiometric dating?

At first, ages were assigned to different rock strata by use of the Theory of Evolution itself. Evolutionists assumed that more complicated forms of life developed from simpler forms. They also assumed that this took millions and millions of years. So different rock strata were often identified by the fossils they contained, and ages were simply assigned.

Today the method scientists use to help estimate the age of Earth and of rock strata is radiometric dating. Some kinds of radioactive materials "decay" (break down) at a very slow rate. This means that a certain percent of different radioactive elements slowly turn into other elements. Carbon 14 turns into carbon 12. Uranium turns into thorium and then into lead. Rubidium turns into strontium.

Scientists have tried to calculate the age of fossils and rocks by mea-

THE GEOLOGIC COLUMN

ERA	PERIOD	AGES IN MILLIONS OF YEARS BEFORE PRESENT
CENOZOIC	QUATERNARY	
		2
	TERTIARY	
		65
MESOZOIC	CRETACEOUS	
		135
	JURASSIC	
		190
	TRIASSIC	
		225
PALEOZOIC	PERMIAN	
		260
	PENNSYLVANIAN	
		325
	MISSISSIPPIAN	
		345
	DEVONIAN	
		400
	SILURIAN	
		430
	ORDOVICIAN	
		500
	CAMBRIAN	
		600
PRE-CAMBRIAN	LATE PRECAMBRIAN	2500
	EARLY PRECAMBRIAN	4800

NO LIFE

The kinds of fossils shown are typically found in these rock strata. But often rocks and fossils do not fit this pattern. And there is no way to be sure that the dates assigned are correct.

suring the amount of these elements. They then figure out how long it would take for the source material, carbon 14, uranium or rubidium, to decay into carbon 12, thorium or lead, or strontium. This figure gives scientists what they believe is the approximate age of the fossil or rock being dated.

We can understand how radiometric dating works if we imagine a large hotel in which there are 1,000 people. You stand outside and notice that every day at noon one adult woman comes out of the hotel, and a young girl goes in to take her place.

After you have watched this for ten days and are sure that only one exchange a day is made, you figure out a way to tell how long the people have been in the hotel! You will go inside and count both the women and young girls.

Let's suppose you do go in and that you count 600 women and 400 young girls. How long will the people have been in the hotel? Why, exactly 400 days.

How do you know? You weren't there when the women went into the hotel. But you know that every day one young girl changes places with one woman. If there are 400 young girls, then it took 400 days for the exchange, and the group went into the hotel 400 days ago.

This is how radiometric dating works. The original element is *exchanged* for another element at a fixed rate. If you know how many exchanges have taken place, then you can tell when the process started.

Because carbon 14 breaks down relatively quickly, it cannot be used to measure times over 10,000 or 15,000 years. But scientists have

used rubidium, which decays very slowly, to measure times they believe go back as far as 4.5 billion years!

What's *wrong* with radiometric dating?

In some cases radiometric dating seems to work as those who believe in Evolution predict. But in other cases the methods give very different results than are expected. Actually, there are many reasons why radiometric dating cannot be considered reliable.

Think back to that hotel. We decided that the group entered the hotel 400 days ago. We reached this conclusion by counting the young girls, thinking that the exchange was one young girl for one woman per day. If there were 400 children, we reasoned the group entered the hotel 400 days ago.

The problem is, to reach this conclusion we had to make several assumptions. That is, we had to suppose that certain things are true which we do not *know* are true.

First, we assumed that the 1,000 people who went into the hotel were all adult women. But what if when they went in, there were 800 women and 200 young girls? In that case our figure of 400 days would be wrong. The group would have been in the hotel for only 200 days.

Scientists *assume* that originally the material in a radiometric sample was carbon 14 or rubidium or whatever. What if originally only part was carbon 14 and part was already carbon 12? What if originally part of the material being measured was rubidium and part was already strontium? Since we do not know what was there originally, the dates may be very far from correct.

Second, remember that we watched the hotel for just ten days. We saw one exchange take place each day. So we *assumed* that the rate of exchange had not changed since the group went into the hotel.

But what if, before we started watching, *four* young girls changed places with four women each day? Then again we would be wrong about when the group entered the hotel.

This too is a problem for radiometric dating. Experiments have shown that carbon 14, for instance, does change into carbon 12 at different rates, depending on factors like heat and radiation. Also, we now know that high electric voltages definitely change the rate of decay of many elements.

So while carbon dating seems relatively accurate up to its 10,000 to 15,000 year limit, there are serious reasons to doubt the evolutionists' confidence that the Earth's rocks and fossils *must* be of great age.

Mysteries of the Earth that cast doubt on scientists' present theories can't be explained away by the notion that "given enough time" anything could have happened.

From the beginning?

One of the mysteries that casts doubt on evolutionists' picture of Earth's past is soil. People who believe in the Theory of Evolution think of Earth's crust and of life itself as developing over billions of years. Yet the nature of Earth's soil suggests that it *couldn't* have happened that way!

Perhaps the most important thing about Earth's crust is that much of it is covered with soil. Soil is the fine earth on land surfaces, that contains the materials needed to support plant and animal life.

The soil is made up in part of minerals washed out of rocks, and of weathered rock itself that has been broken down into small grains. But alone, such rock material is sterile. Plants can't grow in it; animals can't live on it. It will not support life.

To support life, soil must also contain organic matter. What is "organic matter"? It is material that comes from or is made up of once-living things. So soil must contain elements that come from plants and animals.

In fact, soil also must contain vast numbers of *living* organisms, from single-celled bacteria to tiny animals. The *Encyclopedia Britannica* says that a square foot of rich soil may contain up to one billion organisms!

These tiny living things help to break down the decaying bodies of plants and animals that have died. The chemicals in the dead organic matter will be used again to grow the plants and animals that replace the ones that died. Also, soil bacteria take nitrogen from rocks and air and release it in forms that can be used by plants.

If we look at the surface of the Earth and ask what is necessary for it to support life, we have to give this answer. We need soil made of weathered rock, and we need the chemicals that water washes from the rocks. We need air and water. But soil also must contain organic matter. And soil must have millions of tiny living organisms in it if anything is to grow.

This poses a difficult problem for those who believe in the slow evolution of Earth's surface and of living things. Where did the soil that living things need in order to exist come from before there were living things to fill the soil with organic matter?

The only possible explanation is that Earth and life did not develop as scientists now think. When God created the world, he must have covered its continents with soil already filled with the living creatures that Earth must have in order to support life.

What was Earth like when it was created?

People have tried in different ways to calculate the age of the Earth. As we've seen, each approach has its problems. We really can't be certain whether God created the Earth millions of years ago, or merely thousands. The Bible does not tell us how old Earth is. And evidence from Earth's surface is uncertain.

But there is another question we should ask. What was Earth like when God created it? Was Earth just empty rock, or was it much as it is today, a watery world filled with many different kinds of plants and animals? Certainly the nature of soil provides a strong indi-

Millions of germ-sized organisms live in Earth's soil. The effect of this organic matter is important in the cycle of plant life. And we depend on plants for our lives.

cation that Earth was not too different then from now.

Earth has known cataclysms: perhaps meteorite strikes, certainly the great Flood described in Genesis. But original Earth was probably not at all as those who believe in the Theory of Evolution imagine. Many of Earth's features may be thought of as present at creation!

We might raise a similar question about Adam. What was Adam like when he was created? Was he created as a baby? Or was Adam created grown up, looking like an adult perhaps about thirty years old? It's clear from the Bible that Adam was created as an adult. He may have *seemed* thirty years old the day after he was created!

Some Christians argue that our Earth was also created "grown up." There were trees that looked as if they had grown for years. Light from distant stars was created too, traveling to Earth just as if it had been on its way for billions of years. If God created our world much as it is today, how could anyone possibly tell how old it is?

While some have said that such a creation would be deceptive, this isn't necessarily so. After all, God has provided much evidence of creation. Who can tell what mysteries might now be explained if evolutionists had not rejected God, and scientists did not try to explain all things without him.

Some scientists who have become convinced that the Bible is scientifically correct now study the Bible to find "leads" or "clues" about other possible truths God has revealed about his universe.

Will the mysteries ever be solved?

Human beings probably will always study our Earth and try to learn about it. Astronomers will study the stars and galaxies in the heavens. More and more will be learned about our solar system and the sun. More will be learned about Earth's atmosphere and its crust. More will be learned about the seas. Some of the things that appear to be mysteries today may be explained in the future. But always, new mysteries will be uncovered.

Always, too, people will come up with new theories to try to explain what they learn. This is how science has always worked. As more and more is learned, old theories change and new theories are developed. What "most scientists believe" in one generation—like the belief of scientists in 1915 that Earth's continents have not moved—is often revised by the next generation.

So it's foolish to believe something today just because "most scientists say" or "most scientists believe" it is true. We Christians can't be sure about our scientific theories either. Just because a Christian scientist thinks something is true does not prove it. All scientists work with theories. No scientist can say his theory is a fact.

The Bible is not a science book and does not try to explain scientific mysteries. What the Bible does do is to tell us that this universe and life itself didn't just happen! It tells us that God made the universe. God created the heavens and filled space with galaxies of stars. God shaped our Earth, making it a home for living creatures. God created all living things. And, most special of all, God created human beings for him to love and for them to love him.

Is it foolish to believe in God when we can't solve all the mysteries that exist in our universe? Not at all! In fact, the more we learn about our universe and the more mysteries we uncover, the more we realize that it is foolish *not* to believe in God.

Despite many things we can't explain, a study of our world convinces us that the universe, our planet and life itself, really could not "just happen." In the beginning, there *was* God!

Just For Fun

1 Do you think that the age of the Earth makes much difference to a person who believes in creation?

Why or why not? Does it make a difference to someone who believes in the Theory of Evolution? Why or why not?

2 After reading this chapter, what would you think if you saw this headline in a newspaper: "Fossil Remains of Two 225-million-year-old Crows Found!"?

3 Look on a map of the world. How many mountain ranges seem to lie along the edges of continents? How many lie in the middle?

4 Some of the rock formations on Mount Everest, the highest mountain on Earth, are sedimentary rocks formed by moving water. Can you think of any way those rocks might have gotten there?

5 If someone claims that radiometric dating has proven Earth is billions of years old, invite him to read *Critique of Radiometric Dating* by H. S. Slusher (Institute for Creation Research, 1987).

HOW LIFE BEGAN

Now the earth was formless and empty, darkness was over the surface of the deep, and the Spirit of God was hovering over the waters.

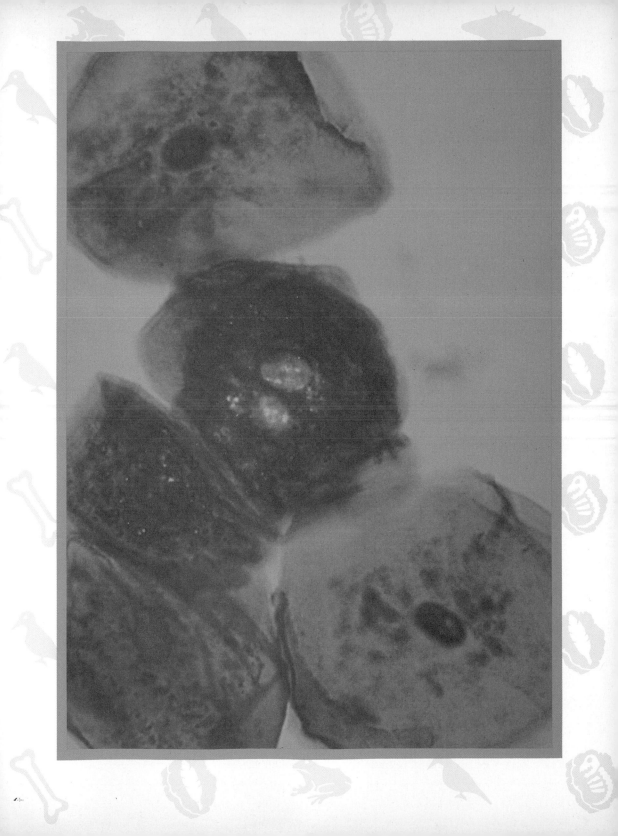

HOW SCIENCE WORKS

Most people have a great respect for scientists and what they say. But are scientists always right? Before we can evaluate what scientists say about how life began, we need to understand what "science" is and how it works. Perhaps the best way to find out is to become a scientist yourself. Follow the suggestions in this chapter, and think like a scientist!

Let's suppose you and a friend, Red, have an argument.

Red says, "I'm a better runner than you are! Redheaded people are good runners. Why, redheads are the best runners in the world! Any redhead can beat any blond any day!"

Now, you *can* just sit there and argue. Sometimes people like to argue and don't want to find out what is right.

But Red has made some statements that can be tested. In scientific language, he has stated *hypotheses*. And these can be *falsified*. Red has claimed that something is generally or always true (his idea that redheads are faster runners). And you can figure out ways to test this idea to see if it is supported by evidence. If the evidence is against his idea, that idea or theory (hypothesis) is probably false.

Look at some of the statements Red made. What experiments can you think of that might provide evidence that Red is wrong? Cover the right side of the chart (pg. 57) and in the middle write ways to test each of Red's hypotheses.

Are the world's best runners redheads?

TESTING RED'S THEORIES

HIS HYPOTHESES	MY TESTS	POSSIBLE TEST IDEAS
1. I can run faster than you can.		Race with Red. Find out best time of each in past races.
2. Redheads are the best runners.		Find out hair color of champion runners. Line up lots of redheads and other people and see which group does best. Line up all the people in the world and see if redheads do best.
3. Any redhead can beat any blond any day.		Race any redhead against any blond. Race all redheads against all blonds.

How scientists test their ideas

When you thought up experiments to get evidence that Red is wrong, you began to think like a scientist. This is basically what the scientific method involves. Someone has an idea. He plans and conducts experiments to get information that will show whether or not the idea is correct.

Some experiments you think up will be hard to conduct. In testing Red's idea, it's impossible to line up every person in the world for a race. So you need to decide ahead of time what experiments you *can* conduct that will provide strong evidence for or against Red's idea.

It might seem that Red's claims can be falsified easily. "I can run faster than you" seems easy enough to prove wrong. You just run a race!

"Redheads are the best runners" seems harder. Still, with a little research you might check this hypothesis. You might go to track meets and observe the races. You might buy a track magazine and check hair color in photos of winners. You might find a book on track champions and see if their hair color is mentioned there.

"Any redhead can beat any blond in any race" also seems easy to falsify. Simply race the fastest blond you know against a redhead you think is slow. Or race ten redheads against ten blonds. If *any* blond wins, that hypothesis of Red's seems wrong.

It seems that the scientific approach gives us a quick and easy way to test what people believe.

It's not really that easy

Sometimes when we argue with people like Red, we get upset because they don't seem to play fair. Let's suppose you've said to Red, "You think you can run faster than me? Prove it!"

You start off together, and sure enough, you beat Red to the corner! "There," you say. "Redheads don't run so fast! I beat you. That proves you're wrong."

But Red, leaning against a tree to catch his breath, keeps on arguing! "I didn't mean I could run faster than you to the corner *today*. I've got a cold and can't run as fast as I usually do."

Now, this doesn't seem fair at all! Red said *he* could run faster. You raced and you won. Red was wrong. So how can he keep on arguing with you?

In scientific terms you conducted an experiment, observed the results, and those results falsified his hy-

pothesis. The facts seem to show that his idea is wrong. Shouldn't Red just give up and admit that redheads aren't faster?

But Red's claims—that he can run faster and that any redhead can beat a person with another hair color— are just *hypotheses*. Each hypothesis is rooted in a more basic idea. That basic idea is the underlying *theory*.

What then is the theory that lies behind Red's claims? Red believes that hair color is related to running ability.

What happens when hypotheses drawn from a basic theory are tested? And what can scientists' experiments prove?

Let's go back to Red's refusal to give up his theory in spite of his defeat. Even though you beat Red in a race, your win did *not* prove that redheads aren't better runners. Even if most of the champion runners of the past were blond or had dark hair, Red might still be right. Red-haired people still could be better runners!

Then why wouldn't there be more redheaded track stars? Possibly because there are many more people with blond or dark hair than there are redheads. Out of 100 people, 3 might have red hair. There is a better chance of having a very fast runner from a group of 97 than from a group of 3!

So possibly Red is right and the *average* red-haired person *is* faster than the average blond or brunette. None of the experiments we've thought of will falsify *that*.

To really test Red's theory we need better experiments. For instance, we need to make sure that the only thing to affect the results of our experiments is hair color. Maybe Red had a big meal before you raced. Maybe he drank too much water. Maybe he had a sore heel. Maybe your legs are longer than Red's and if your legs were the same length he would have won.

A scientist has to set up experiments very carefully. He or she will want to have the runners run on the same track, in the same kind of shoes, with the same training, and under the same variety of weather conditions! The scientist will want to adjust for weight and height. Also, the scientist will repeat the experiment many times.

How many times should races be run under each condition to be sure of the results? One? Ten? A hundred? One hundred races may seem like too many. But suppose you and Red raced one hundred times, and Red won seven of the first ten. You might win seventy-five of the next ninety!

So good scientists need to be extremely careful about the experiments they set up to gather evidence for or against a theory. They know that no experiment can guard against *everything* that might affect its results.

Developing better theories

Let's suppose you've run a number of races against Red and have even conducted other well-planned experiments. You take your results to Red and show him the evidence. "There," you say. "Redheads don't run so fast."

But Red keeps on arguing! "Just because you held a bunch of races doesn't mean that redheads aren't faster most of the time. Besides, you ran short races. I meant that redheads are better in *longer* races."

Now, this doesn't seem fair at all. You now have solid evidence against each of Red's hypotheses. Shouldn't Red just abandon his theory?

Well, if both you and Red want to go about this scientifically, Red should *not* give up! Actually, in science this kind of thing happens all the time. When results of experiments don't turn out, scientists are often led to *modify a theory* instead of abandoning it.

Most theories need to be modified. They need to be changed for better definition. Remember, you and Red started to argue about "running fast." But neither of you said what

"Water boils at 212°" has been proven many times. But here water will boil at a much lower temperature. How should we make our statement so it will always be true?

("*Water boils at 212° at sea level.*")

"running fast" meant exactly.

Did Red mean run fast for a short distance (a sprint), or did he mean run fast for a middle distance (such as a mile) or run fast over a very long distance (say, for ten miles)?

The evidence you gathered in your experiments may lead Red to modify his theory even more. What does redhead mean? Does it mean *very* red hair, or does "red hair" include reddish brown? Is his theory about redheaded girls and women or just redheaded boys and men? Is the theory about redheads between five and eight years old or redheads between eighteen and twenty-one? It's possible that redheaded children run faster, but teens or adults don't. Or that older redheads run faster, even though they didn't as children.

Suddenly something that seemed very simple and very easy to test has become quite complicated!

Actually while learning about things "scientifically" might seem easy, the "scientific approach" *is* very involved. And most basic theories are very hard to test. All too often theories scientists have accepted as true have been rejected later! Just because a person is a scientist, or gathers information in a scientific way, his or her theories will not necessarily be right!

Good science and bad science

"Science" is an approach to learning things. The scientific approach tests theories, using experiments and gathering all sorts of data (informa-tion) that will suggest whether the theories should be accepted or rejected.

Sometimes rejected theories have been accepted later. Very often theories that everyone accepted have been rejected later on.

The point is, a theory is just a belief until it's *proven* to be something else. It can be proven "true" and become a *fact*. Or it can be proven "false" and become *fiction*.

Copernicus had a theory that the Earth and other planets circle around the sun. In his day most people accepted the idea that Earth was the center of the solar system. After all, the sun seems to circle the Earth every day!

Scientists of that day made a pre-

What's wrong here? What theory might it seem to falsify? How can you explain what you observe and retain your theory, too?

(Light travels in a straight line. This beam seems bent, but maybe there is a mirror behind the rock that reflects the beam.)

diction designed to falsify Copernicus' theory. If the theory is correct, they said, the planet Venus will come closer to Earth, and then move away from it. If that happens, the light

With larger telescopes, astronomers have discovered that earlier theories about how stars form may be wrong. New facts nearly always bring changes in scientific theories.

from Venus will brighten, and then get more dim. When people looked at Venus, they couldn't see any difference in brightness. So they claimed Copernicus was wrong! He had a theory, and there was a scientific way to falsify it.

But Copernicus was right! The planets do circle the sun. What had happened? Venus does get brighter and dimmer, but this change cannot be seen by the human eye. Today we have instruments sensitive enough to measure the difference.

Was the experiment proposed by those who doubted Copernicus bad science? Not really. When they assumed that one could tell the difference in brightness with the naked eye, they made a mistake any scientist might make.

In 1910 scientists believed in what is called the Nebular Theory. This theory said that our sun and the other stars evolved from hot, swirling gases as they cooled in space. Astronomers looking through telescopes saw great spirals in the sky that *looked* like swirling gas. Most astronomers viewed this as evidence for the Nebular Theory. After all, they could actually see swirling gases that would one day become stars.

Then, in California a new 100-inch telescope was pointed toward the stars. Now the astronomers realized that the spirals they saw in space were not gas, but were galaxies, made up of a billion stars! What scientists had thought—that swirling gas clouds rotate in space—was not a fact at all!

Good science constantly searches for information and is open to new information. When scientists have wrong information or not enough information, the theories they accept are likely to be wrong. Good science doesn't jump to conclusions. "Bad science" was to reject Copernicus' theory on so little evidence!

Bad science can mean poorly conducted experiments. But most often the difference between good science and bad science lies in the conclusions a scientist draws. A good scientist will be cautious, while a less capable scientist will jump to conclusions.

The "ruling theory trap"

What do scientists do when they have accepted a theory and just don't want to give it up? What if our friend Red simply doesn't want to give up his theory about redheaded people being good runners? Then, no matter how much evidence seems to falsify his hypotheses, he might still insist his theory is right!

To keep from abandoning his theory, Red can keep changing his theory just slightly. Red might say it is very red-haired people who are fast. Your experiments weren't conducted with people whose hair was red enough. Or he might say it is young red-haired boys and redheaded teenage girls who run fast. Red might accept the results of races redheads win as *valid* evidence, and argue that when they lost there was something wrong with the experiment.

If Red keeps on refusing to accept our evidence, or modifies his theory every time we get new evidence that he is wrong, we may decide that for some reason or other, Red just *wants* to think of redheads as good runners. (You can probably think of at least one reason why this might be a favorite theory of Red's!)

Red has fallen into the "ruling theory trap." Red's thinking is so powerfully affected by his theory that his judgment is affected. Red cannot think objectively about the data because his judgment is controlled (ruled) by his theory!

In science a person should remain objective and not prefer one theory to another. But scientists are human and often want to believe a theory despite the evidence. And scientists can be prejudiced against others' theories, too. This may lead a scientist to consciously or unconsciously accept evidence that supports his theory and to ignore evidence that doesn't fit the theory.

This is what the scientists who opposed Copernicus did. From just one piece of evidence against his theory, they jumped to the conclusion that it must be wrong. Those scientists, just like Red, were caught in the ruling theory trap.

It's something like this for scientists who want to believe in the Theory of Evolution. Most evolutionists really *want* to believe that everything "just happened" by chance. Of course, scientists who believe that God created all things want to believe in creation. So both Evolution and creation are "ruling theories." It is very hard for a creationist to convince a scientist who accepts the Theory of Evolution that his favorite theory is false, in spite of the evidence on the creationist's side!

Charles Darwin wrote about the evolution of all living creatures, and most scientists accepted his theory. Early evolutionists predicted that they would find fossil evidence of gradual change from one kind of animal to another in the bones or fossil bodies found in Earth's rocks. That prediction has proved false. But people did not reject the Theory of Evolution.

Research has shown that even slight mutations are almost always harmful. Thousands of experiments have produced no clear evidence of beneficial mutations or shown how such mutations could be responsible for the variety of living things. But scientists still have not rejected the Theory of Evolution. Even now they are trying to figure out some way Evolution might have taken place.

Evolutionists insist that living things "just happened" to start up from the dead rocks and minerals and waters of our planet. Yet today, as we'll see later, strong evidence shows that life surely *did not* begin that way. Yet evolutionists argue that it *must* have and that some day they will learn how. When people hold a ruling theory, they are likely to reject evidence against that theory, no matter how strong the evidence is.

Is scientific proof possible?

Could you prove to someone who believes in the Theory of Evolution that he or she is wrong? Probably not. Why?

There is never "enough" evidence. You can prove that water boils at sea level at 212° F by repeated, controlled experiments. The doubters can see for themselves. But no one can go back and watch creation or experiment with history.

When it comes to issues like Evolution and creation, we have to rea-

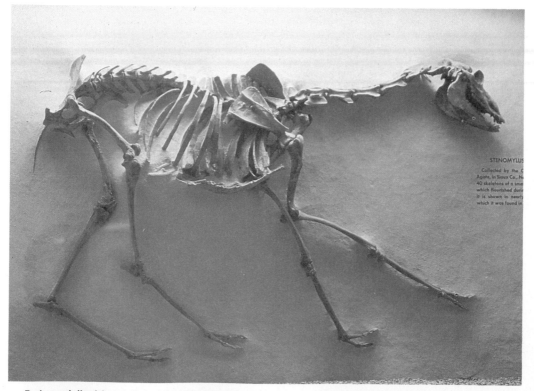

STENOMYLUS

Collected by the C
Agate, in Sioux Co., N
40 skeletons of a sma
which flourished durir
It is shown in nearly
which it was found in

Early evolutionists predicted that they would find fossils showing a series of changes proving that fish turned into amphibians or reptiles turned into birds. We now have hundreds of thousands of fossils, but none reveals the kind of changes to demonstrate the Theory of Evolution.

son from circumstantial evidence. There is much we can learn about the universe and about Earth and about living creatures by gathering evidence. But we never have *all* the information we need. Some data is always missing. So people must reason from *part* of the evidence, not *all* of the evidence. Yet the evidence we have makes it clear that the theory of creation is far better than the Theory of Evolution!

There are things we will never know for sure or understand completely through the methods of science. How and when did God create the universe? What exactly happened on Earth in the past? These are questions we will never be able to answer for sure.

However, we can look at evidence that has convinced scientists who are Christians that there is more "scientific" evidence *for* creation than against it! And we can look at much evidence *against* the Theory of Evolution.

But, in the end we do not believe in creation just because it is more likely scientifically. We believe in creation because we believe in God and because we trust what God has revealed to us in the Bible.

But it is important to realize one thing. When some claim that the Theory of Evolution is a scientific fact, they are wrong. Evolution is just a theory. And it is a ruling theory, that is held in spite of solid scientific evidence *against* it!

Just For Fun

1 Choose one of these theories and decide what evidence might prove or disprove it. (a) Girls are smarter than boys. (b) Girls grow faster than boys. (c) Most women are older than their husbands.

2 What could you say to a teacher who says that the Theory of Evolution is a fact?

3 Here is a statement from a geology textbook. What is the writer saying? "No scientific report is ever more than a progress report. It is something someone has found out and that someone else will modify, expand, or replace. This has been true in geology as in all the sciences."

4 What might be fun about being a scientist? What might not be fun?

5 Do you think "scientific evidence" can prove creation? Why or why not?

7 "LIFE" IN A TEST TUBE?

People who believe the Theory of Evolution think that life began billions of years ago as certain chemicals happened to mix together under just the right conditions. Scientists have conducted experiments that imitate those conditions. No one has come close to making life. What would have had to happen to make life? And what are the chances that life could come from *any* mix of non-living matter?

For hundreds of years people did believe that living things came from non-living things. They thought spoiled meat turned into white worms. They thought mud turned into frogs and old rags became rats.

Then a man named Franceso Redi conducted an experiment to test that theory. He put meat into two jars. One of the jars was covered with fine cloth, and the other jar was left open. The meat in both jars spoiled. But only the meat in the open jar developed white worms!

Redi repeated the experiment and found that the same thing happened. Then he noticed that the meat in the open jar had flies crawling over it, but there were no flies on the meat in the covered jar. Redi studied the flies carefully and realized that they were laying eggs on the spoiled meat! The white worms came from the eggs and, in time, grew into flies.

Other early scientists conducted other careful experiments and came to an important conclusion. *Life can come only from other life.*

In the world as we know it today, there is no way that life can simply start up on its own, coming from non-living matter.

Either/or

Scientists agree that life only comes from living things in today's world. Yet the Theory of Evolution insists that millions of years ago life sprang from non-living chemicals. One famous scientist, Dr. Robert Jastrow, says there are only two choices.

Either life was created on the Earth by the will of a being outside the grasp of scientific understanding [God], or it evolved on our planet spontaneously, through chemical reactions occurring in non-living matter lying on the surface of the planet.[1]

This makes our choice very simple. We must either believe that life just happened to begin or else believe that God created life. If we can show that life *could not* happen through chemical reactions occurring in non-living matter lying on the surface of our planet, then we have evidence that God *must have* created life!

Suppose that you have a dollar in one hand. You ask a friend to guess which. He says, "The right hand!" Now, either he is right, or he is wrong. And, if he is wrong, then the dollar must be in your left hand! As soon as you show that one of only two possible choices is wrong, then the other choice must be right!

It's like this with the appearance of life. There are only two choices. God created life, or life started by chance. If we can show that life did not start up in some chance process, the other choice—that God created beings—must be right!

What do Evolutionists think happened?

Scientists who believe the Theory of Evolution of life know it could not happen unless Earth was once very different than it is now. They picture early Earth as molten rock, giving off volcanic gases like methane, carbon dioxide, ammonia and water vapor. Some think thousands of meteorites struck Earth from space, bringing millions of tons of carbon. Perhaps water vapor was formed by gases from volcanoes.

Evolutionists think that Earth was once a hot, dead planet and that as it cooled, life began. They say chemicals were mixed in shallow pools and just happened to come alive.

However, after hundreds of millions of years they suppose that Earth cooled. Rain fell on the black, jumbled, empty rocks of Earth. Finally water lay in shallow seas and in millions of pools and streams.

Because there was no free oxygen in the air then, and therefore no ozone layer, powerful rays of ultraviolet light from the sun struck the water and the chemicals that were dissolved in it and caused change.

No scientist can say just *how* it is supposed to have happened, but evolutionists think that carbon and ammonia and other atoms began to link up, to form the chemical combinations necessary for living cells. Then, somehow, these chemicals formed more complex structures. Finally, somehow, just the right chemicals were all together in the right place, and a living cell formed! This living cell reproduced itself from the chemicals in the water around it and, from this beginning—a single cell— all the plants and animals on Earth developed.

Stanley Miller's experiment

In 1953 a college science student named Stanley Miller decided to conduct an experiment. He designed a system of glass tubes and bottles to reproduce conditions evolutionists thought once existed on Earth. He put water and gases into his invention. He heated the liquid and used electric sparks instead of ultraviolet rays to jolt the chemicals. What happened seemed exciting. His experiment actually produced some of the amino acids and other simple compounds found in living things! The newspapers reported that Miller had nearly made "life in a test tube."

But while amino acids are found in living things, they are only building blocks. Amino acids are not themselves living things. It's as if a person found three or four bricks in the back yard, and the newspaper headlines read "Local man engineers 50 story skyscraper!" There's a long way to go from having building blocks to having a completed building.

Miller's experiment did make some of the amino acids found in living things. But this does not mean he showed how living things began. How do we know? First, all the right amino acids are found in dead bodies—but the bodies are still dead. Just having the right amino acids doesn't make something alive.

Second, not all the amino acids needed by living things were formed in Miller's experiment. At least three key amino acids have not been made in the many experiments conducted by scientists since 1953.

Third, many acids *harmful* to the development of life are formed in experiments like Miller's! These experiments produce what one evolutionist scientist calls "hopelessly complex 'gunks.'" The chemicals in the "gunks" would have *kept* life from developing, not helped it develop!

So Miller's experiment did *not* create "life in a test tube." It did not even come close to making a single living cell. Such experiments have shown just how unbelievable the notion of the chemical evolution of life really is.

What is in a cell?

How complex is a single cell? One scientist who believes in Evolution, J. Keosian, says that the simplest cell "is an intricate ... unit of harmoniously coordinated parts and chemical pathways. Its spontaneous assembly out of the environment, granting the unlikely simultaneous presence together of all the parts, is not a believable possibility."[2]

Even so, Keosian and other evolutionists believe that somehow that single cell *did* form spontaneously.

But *why* is the forming of a single cell so unbelievable? It's unbelievable partly because there are so many different kinds of chemicals in living cells.

Amino acids. Some 20 different kinds of amino acids are needed for the protein in living cells. Even after thirty years of experiments, three key amino acids have not been made chemically even in experiments especially designed to produce them!

Also, the way *some* amino acids must be made in the test tube (using heat, gases, electricity or ultraviolet rays) will destroy *other* amino acids. Many are destroyed by heat. Others are broken down by oxygen or by other acids. Even if Earth had ever been as evolutionists imagine, the amino acids that might have formed then would quickly have been destroyed. Without the protection provided by being in a living cell, amino acids could never have come together to evolve further!

Lipids. These fatty materials make up about 10% of the simplest cells. No one has been able to make lipids chemically. They are only produced by life.

Porphyrin. This is an important molecule in hemoglobin, the element in red blood cells that carries oxygen. Evolutionists realize that there *must* have been porphyrins for life to survive. Without porphyrins, oxygen breaks down the other chemicals in a cell. But porphyrinlike chemicals can only be made when there is free oxygen available.

If amino acids can only be made when there is *no* free oxygen in the atmosphere, and porphyrins can only be made when there *is* free oxygen, *then these things needed by every cell could not have existed together to form the first cell*! What's more, many of these compounds are antagonistic. They will combine and destroy each other—anywhere *except* within a living cell.

Polynucleotides. These complex chemicals are found in DNA and RNA, linked together in groups of as many as 4,500 units. DNA is the "code" that cells use to reproduce the proteins of which cells are composed. That "code" also tells the cells how to make more DNA.

What does this mean? Simply that to *make* DNA, you have to *have* DNA in the first place! You have to have the DNA code within the cell before you can make more DNA code. Without the complete code in the first place, there is no way to make the code necessary for every living cell!

There are many more elements found in living cells that we could look at. But we really don't need to list them. The more scientists learn about cells, the more complex and special they appear to be.

No one who studies the living cell can explain how life could begin from non-living things. In fact, the more scientists learn, the clearer it is that life from non-living chemicals simply *could not* just happen.

How do we know it couldn't just happen?

People who still believe in the Theory of Evolution say that, given enough time, *anything* can happen. They think the Earth is billions of

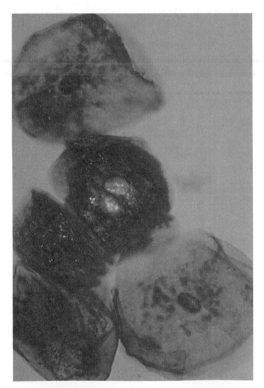

Even the smallest of living cells is made up of many different chemicals, all linked in unbelievably complex relationships.

years old and that billions of years is enough time. Besides, no matter how unlikely the chance beginning of life may seem, life *did* begin. And, since these evolutionists do not believe in God, they are sure it *must* have "just happened."

Is there any way to tell if something can happen by chance? Mathematicians work out what is called *probability theory*. Using probability theory it is possible to tell just how likely it is for something to happen.

If you've ever looked at contest forms, you may have read something like this: "Your chance of winning the Grand Prize in this contest is 1 in 329,870,000." That means if the same contest were run over 329 million times, you'd have a good chance to win! Someone may win the contest you enter. But the chances are very, very small that the winner will be you!

Probability theory can tell you many other things, too. Suppose you take ten coins and flip each of them. How many do you suppose will turn up heads, and how many will turn up tails?

If you flip the ten coins enough times (say, 1000 times each), probability theory tells us that about half the flips will turn up heads and half will turn up tails.

How many times would you have to flip the coins for all ten to turn up heads at the same time? Probability theory tells you how to find out. You multiply 10 x 9 x 8 x 7 x 6 x 5 x 4 x 3 x 2 x 1. What does that work out to? To have all ten coins turn up heads at the same time, you would need to flip the coins an average of 4,132,800 times.

This is a polarized light micrograph of crystals of the amino acid arginine. A protein molecule consists of anywhere from a hundred to several thousand amino acids.

How long would that take you? Well, if you flipped all ten coins twice each minute and worked ten hours a day, every day, it would take you almost ten years of coin flipping to be sure that all ten would turn up heads just once!

Of course, if you were to place the coins heads up on purpose, it wouldn't take you long at all!

Whenever we have a number of things that need to happen at the same time, we can use probability theory to find out how likely it is they will happen together by chance.

One of the most amazing puzzles in biology is the fact that proteins in living things are "left-handed." Proteins are long, slender threads 500 times too thin to be seen under even a good microscope. They are made up of chains of amino acids. There are between 100 and 50,000 different amino acid links in each protein chain. There are an average of at least 400 amino acids in the smallest known living things.

Each of these amino acids is made up of different atoms attached to one side of another atom. Each different amino acid has a different side group. And all the amino acids in living things have their side group on the *left* side!

Yet when scientists make amino acids in their laboratories, half the acids produced are right-handed! So if the amino acids form by chance, half of them are right-handed and half are left-handed.

What if we use probability theory to find out how likely it is that the *smallest possible living thing* would just happen to have only left-handed amino acids? Well, there is one chance in ten—followed by 123 zeros!

A professor at the Massachusetts Institute of Technology has estimated that all the protein molecules that have ever existed on Earth is only ten followed by 52 zeros. This means that there *is no real chance at all that even one protein with all left-handed amino acids could ever have "just happened" to come into existence*!

But there are other things that are special about the proteins in living creatures, too. The average protein in the smallest known living thing has about 400 amino acid links. And each amino acid link must be in the right order.

It is something like the alphabet. To make words, the letters in the alphabet must be in a particular order.

If the letters in "letter" are out of order (as "teertl"), those letters don't make a meaningful word. In even small proteins, about 400 amino acid links (letters) have to be in just the right order—or the protein does not work!

What is the probability of an amino acid chain 400 units long happening by chance? The answer is, one chance in ten—followed by 240 zeros!

One mathematician figured that, even if chemicals combined 150 thousand trillion times faster than they do in living things, and used all the chemical atoms on earth, there would be only one chance in ten followed by 161 zeros that a single usable protein could have been

This model illustrates the structure of the DNA molecule. The genetic information is determined by the arrangement of these pairs along the molecule.

produced by chance in the history of the Earth!

But living cells have more than proteins. They also contain DNA, that code necessary for living things to reproduce. If all the atoms in the universe were made into the chemicals from which DNA is formed, and they were put together again and again at eight trillion chains a second, would it be possible to have a single DNA gene (a code carrier) come about by chance? Only if we have ten—followed by 147 zeros—years!

How long is that? Another mathematician imagined a tiny snail moving so slowly that it took 3,810,000,000,000,000,000 years to travel one inch. If the snail carried one atom across the thirty billion light years of our universe, it would take him about four x ten—followed by 125 zeros—years! The mathematician explains, "In this leisurely fashion, the little space crawler would have time to carry two x ten followed by twenty-one zeros complete universes, one atom at a time, all the way across the thirty billion light years of the assumed diameter of the cosmos, during the time that chance could be expected to arrange one gene in any usable order, trying at the unbelievable speed noted earlier, using all the atoms of the universe." Dr. James F. Coppedge, the director of the Center for Probability Research in Biology in California, explains the probabilities in his book *Evolution: Possible or Impossible?*

Possible or impossible? The answer is clear. Life simply could not have come about by chance. No matter how much time the Evolutionist thinks passed from Earth's beginning until life evolved, it could not have happened.

Since life could not have begun by chance, it must have been purposely created by God. There is no other choice. If one of only two possible choices could not have happened, the other one did!

So never let anyone convince you that it is foolish or "unscientific" to believe in God. The fact is, scientific evidence shows that it is foolish *not* to believe in God! The evidence truly is on our side!

Just For Fun

1 You can do Redi's experiment (outdoors). Watch to see what happens on uncooked meat in a covered and uncovered jar.

2 "Fish either live out of the water or will die out of water." Can you write five other statements in which one thing or another *must* be true?

3 Explain what the author means when he says either life began by chance or God created life. Why, if we can prove one is *not* true, must the other be true?

4 How many reasons can you find in this chapter that the evolution of life from non-living chemicals couldn't "just happen"?

5 If teachers or friends do not believe it when you say life could not have just happened, ask them to read the book *Chemical Evolution*, by Dr. S. E. Aw, (Master Books, San Diego, CA).

THE MYSTERY OF THE MOTHS

According to the Theory of Evolution, over millions of years living things became more complex and many different varieties of plants and animals developed. But how could this have taken place? Charles Darwin suggested a mechanism he called natural selection. But does natural selection really work the way Darwin thought it did? Today even scientists who believe the Theory of Evolution don't think so.

The moths that changed!

Nearly all biology textbooks, from high school to college, tell the story of the British moths that changed. Before 1848 nearly all peppered moths (*biston betularia*) were a

In just fifty years the lighter pepper moths in England almost died out and were replaced by darker moths. Are changes like this evidence for the Theory of Evolution?

lightly speckled grey. There were a few that were almost black in color, but very few. Then the black form began to increase, until by 1895, 98% of these moths were black! What had happened?

In 1848 there were very few factories in England. The trees in Britain were covered by light-colored lichens [*tiny plants*]. But as factories were built in Britain, smokestacks poured out black smoke and polluted the air. The lichens died out, and the tree trunks showed dark

But what difference did this make to the moths? When the tree trunks were a light color, birds had a harder time seeing light-colored moths that rested on them. But when the tree trunks turned dark, birds could easily see the light grey peppered moths—and ate them. The almost black moths were harder to see against the dark trunks. They survived—and soon there were many more dark moths than light ones. The peppered moths had changed!

Other changes and evolution

Charles Darwin is the man who presented the Theory of Evolution in his book *On the Origin of the Species*. He developed the idea on a voy-

Darwin learned that the tortoises that lived on various islands differed from each other. He thought this was evidence for his Theory of Evolution. But was it?

age around the world on the British ship *Beagle*. On that journey in 1835, Darwin made two discoveries that started him thinking.

On the Galapagos Islands Darwin carefully watched the giant tortoises that lived there. He learned that a person could tell which of several islands a turtle came from by the size, color and thickness of its shell! He also found out that turtles from drier islands fed on tree cactus and had longer necks. Those that lived on wetter islands fed on low-growing plants and had shorter necks.

On those same islands there were twenty-six types of birds, and thirteen of them were finches. The finches also had differences. One type ate ground seeds and had a thick, short beak. Another type fed primarily on insects in trees and had a longer, pointed beak. In fact, there were slight differences in the beak size and shape of each type of finch. And each beak size seemed to be related to the kind of food the bird preferred!

As Darwin thought about this, he realized that each *variation* seemed to enable the bird or turtle to adapt better to its environment. But how did each bird, with its particular differences, develop? It seemed to Darwin that all the finches came from an original stock that had come to the islands. Somehow they must have separated into different subspecies, each with its own special traits.

But how? Darwin knew that offspring are slightly different from their parents. He thought that these minor differences might build up until, after many generations, a kind of bird or animal quite different from the first parents might develop. Dar-

The finches on the various Galapagos Islands had differently shaped beaks, each adapted to what the finches ate. Did these birds all descend from only one kind of original finch? Are the differences evidence for the Theory of Evolution?

win thought that only changes which better helped an animal or plant fit into its environment would be passed on. Darwin called this "natural selection," and it became the keystone of his Theory of Evolution.

Darwin supposed that over the millions of years he believed had passed since the world began, all modern animals had developed from the first living cells as variation was added to variation! And, in many school textbooks, the story of the

moths of England, along with the stories of the turtles and finches of the Galapagos Islands, is still presented as "proof" of Darwin's Theory of Evolution.

The Theory of Evolution and evolution

The word "evolve" simply means to undergo change. When we write "evolution" with a small "e," it simply means that something has experienced a slow or gradual change.

When people speak of Evolution with a capital "E," it means something far different. That Evolution is the theory that (1) life began as a chance combination of non-living chemicals, and (2) that all living things today developed from one-celled creatures, which (3) over millions of years gradually changed into the fish, reptiles, birds and mammals in today's world.

We can all agree that "evolution" with a small "e" happens. But evolution (with a small "e") is *not* proof of Evolution (with a capital "E")!

Darwin did not see this difference. He thought when he discovered the evolution of the tortoises and finches of the Galapagos Island that he had found the secret of Evolution (capital "E").

Darwin believed changes took place in plants and animals all the time. Some of these changes, such as a longer neck or a more pointed beak, helped the organism survive. Some changes hurt rather than helped. The short-necked turtles died out on the dry island because they couldn't reach the cactus fruit. In this way the long neck trait was selected by nature itself! So the mechanism of natural selection seemed to Darwin to explain all differences we see in plant and animal life today.

In 1969 a Time-Life book called *Evolution* used this idea of Darwin's to explain how amphibians evolved from fish. An amphibian is a cold-blooded, smooth-skinned creature, such as a frog, whose young are hatched in water and later develop lungs. According to this book,

> some 365 million years ago, some of these crossopterygian *fish* ventured out on land. It is a plausible guess that they lived in streams which dried in drought of summer into a few scattered pools. Did the fish struggle and flop from one dying pool to another for more water? No one knows, but those fish that were able to stay out of the water for a longer time certainly would have been the survivors and would have left behind offspring with their own greater ability to breathe in the air.

Of course, these *were* fish. Some fish today, like a dogfish, can live out of water for hours, while a bass will die in minutes. But out of water, *any* fish will soon die, for it has no lungs. It will hardly live long enough to mate and lay eggs. And any eggs it does lay have to be laid in running water in order to hatch!

The supposed ability of some fish to live a little longer out of water before they die can hardly explain how finned, scaly creatures could change into smooth-skinned, leggy amphibians who *do* have lungs!

Today few evolutionists believe that Darwin's notion of natural selection can explain the great changes they think took place between such kinds of animals as fish and amphibians or reptiles, or between reptiles and birds or mammals! Yet many textbooks still present evolution (small "e") as evidence for their Theory of Evolution!

What are genes and chromosomes?

Chromosomes are largely composed of DNA and proteins. They are like long thin strings. All along these strings *genes* are found. The genes make up the code for the plant or animal's specific characteristics. Each gene affects some specific trait or body part. They are something like the dots and dashes of the Morse code. The code sequence along the chromosome strings is different for each kind of living creature. Cells in a fish do not contain the code for cells of a bird or cat. Each kind of living creature carries its own code and can reproduce only its own kind. The offspring *must* reproduce the parents' codes.

While no living creature gives birth to a different *kind* of offspring, offspring are not identical to their parents. For instance, people have differently colored hair and eyes. Individuals have differently shaped noses and lips. Some people are short and others are tall. Some are thin and others heavy. But a human being will have human hair and eyes and a human nose and lips. But each individual will be different, in many small ways, from his or her parents, and from other human beings.

We see similar variations in the animal world. There are many different types of dogs. Some are large, some small. Some are hairy, some almost bald. Some dogs have flattened noses, others have long pointed muzzles.

Sometimes there are minor changes in genes, often called "point mutations." Present-day evolutionists, called Neo-Darwinians, think these mutations, along with natural selection, explain the great changes proposed by the Theory of Evolution. But most minor differences we see in presently living creatures are *not* explained by mutation at all!

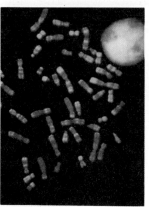
The codes that determine the kind of plant or animal and its nature are all carried in genes that lie along these chromosome strings.

Where do minor differences come from? Scientists who study genes and chromosomes have learned that many differences are built into the genetic material itself. Variable forms of the same gene are called *alleles*. You have the genes for human eyes, but with the *allele* (variation) that

codes for your own distinct eye color.

Because human beings can only have human offspring, the genes you received meant you would be born a human being. But because there are many variations within human genes, you are a unique human being, with your own eye and hair color, nose shape, etc.

In the same way, your pet dog has the basic codes for "dog." But variations in the dog genes determine its fur color and length, and even the breed of dog it is.

Today we know much about the complicated chemical world of genes and chromosomes, but there is much more to be learned. We understand rules that tell which *alleles* persons are most likely to inherit. *But nothing scientists have learned about genetics suggests any way that one kind of animal can have a different kind of offspring.*

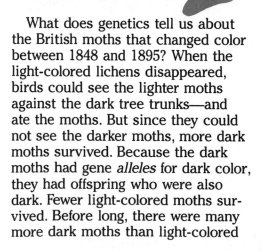

What about those moths?

What does genetics tell us about the British moths that changed color between 1848 and 1895? When the light-colored lichens disappeared, birds could see the lighter moths against the dark tree trunks—and ate the moths. But since they could not see the darker moths, more dark moths survived. Because the dark moths had gene *alleles* for dark color, they had offspring who were also dark. Fewer light-colored moths survived. Before long, there were many more dark moths than light-colored ones. There had been a change (evolution) in the moth population. But this change was due only to variations already built into the moth genes! This kind of change does not support the Theory of Evolution at all!

We can say the same thing about the tortoises and finches on the Galapagos Islands. Gene *alleles* account for the slight changes in the size and shape of the birds' beaks. *Those variations already existed within the possible range of size and shape built into the finch genes.* As more short-beak finches survived, they had more short-beak offspring. As more long-beak finches survived on another island, they had more long-beak offspring. Yet they remained finches, although distinctive island-group differences set them off from each other as finch subspecies. The same holds true for the necks and shell shapes of the turtles.

What is important to notice is that *the evolution of subspecies of finches and turtles did not involve processes that can explain the kind of changes required by the Theory of Evolution.* The finches did not turn into something other than birds. Their beaks did not become mouths with teeth. The genetic code held true. The finches were still finches, and the turtles were still turtles, just as the moths of England remain moths.

Often in writings about Evolution these creatures are used as modern examples of Evolution in progress. But the more we learn about genetics the more we understand how these changes can happen naturally. There was change. But it was evolution (with a small "e"), not Evolution (with a capital "E").

What experiments show

Today evolutionists have realized that evolution is limited by a creature's genetic makeup. The genetic codes of most plants and animals contain a great storehouse of variation and over many generations can produce the kinds of change that Darwin observed. But these changes are simply different combinations of traits that already exist in the creature's genes. A fish cannot suddenly develop the ability to live out of water for the simple reason that this ability is not in its genes.

But evolutionists have not abandoned their theory. They have proposed that *mutations* do explain how one kind of creature can change into another.

A mutation is an error in the genetic code of a particular creature. Mutations are very rare, and when they do occur, they almost always damage the creature. Yet evolutionists argue that once in a great while a change *might* occur which would be helpful. They argue that something like this must have happened and that gradually creatures did change to make the many different forms of life on Earth today.

Yet scientists who hold the Theory of Evolution have experimented for many years with changes in animal features. For sixty years they have worked with a fruit fly called *Drosophila*. There have been thousands of generations of this fruit fly, and experiments have produced many different mutations. Yet scientist Francis

Hitching summed up the results. "Fruit flies refuse to become anything but fruit flies under any circumstances yet devised."[1] Even mutation produces only evolution (small "e") and never the kind of changes required by the Theory of Evolution.

Scientists have also experimented with bacteria. Hundreds of thousands of bacteria generations have been studied and their variations examined. Yet *never* has bacteria been seen to develop into a multicelled form. French evolutionist Pierre-Paul Grasse concluded, "They do not change!"[2]

Many scientists now realize that Darwin's idea of how evolution takes place was wrong. And there is no evidence to support the Neo-Darwinians' idea that major changes in living creatures can take place through small mutations plus natural selection. In fact, even though scientists have tried, they cannot even make one kind of animal change into another.

Were there "hopeful monsters"?

Many evolutionists have now decided that changes from one type of animal to another could not have happened slowly, either by natural selection or by the gradual buildup of mutations. They agree that a reptile could not change slowly into a bird, as Darwin and his modern followers think. During the millions of years it would take while scales turned to feathers and legs became wings, the small, gradual change Darwinism relies on would make it harder for the changing reptile-bird to survive.

Does this mean they have abandoned the Theory of Evolution? Not at all. They simply claim that massive changes must have taken place all at once! One argument for this theory is that the fossil record shows that new kinds of creatures appeared suddenly and then continued basically unchanged over geologic eras.

But what must happen for this kind of change to take place? Well, it must be something like a reptile turning into a bird suddenly—all at once. It is as if a dinosaur were watching its egg hatch and out came a fully developed bird! The animals that evolutionists say must have developed sudden changes have been nicknamed "hopeful monsters." The new creature must at first have seemed a monster, but it had hope for surviving as a totally new form of life. But is this idea of hopeful monsters at all reasonable as a mechanism for explaining how Evolution might have happened? Hardly.

First, there is no evidence at all that anything like a hopeful monster *could* be born. No one has even been able to guess how such a change could take place, since it requires the creation of completely new genetic material. In fact, the more we learn of genetics, the more impossible this kind of sudden change seems. The genetic material that every living creature has is coded to reproduce only its own kind. There is no way for new genetic codes to develop!

This illustration of a bird hatching from a dinosaur "egg" is an example of a "hopeful monster." Evolutionists have suggested hopeful monsters to explain how Evolution between kinds of animals might have taken place.

Next, even if a hopeful monster *were* born, there would have to be another monster of the opposite sex, born in the same place at the same time, for it to reproduce. If appearance of one monster seems impossible, how likely is the appearance of two?

How hard this must be for people who insist on believing the Theory of Evolution. They have no way at all to explain *how* the kind of changes they believe in could possibly have happened!

The old idea, that changes took place gradually through the selection of helpful variations, has been shown to be wrong. Gene *alleles* rather than mutation explain the kind of changes we can observe. All that is left is imagination and the blind conviction that if evolution did not happen slowly, it must have happened in jumps.

What does the Bible say?

In the creation account, the Bible says that God created plants, fish, animals and birds. Carefully read what the Bible says and you will find a very special statement that science has shown to be true!

Then God said, "Let the land produce vegetation: seed-bearing plants and trees on the land that bear fruit with seed in it, according to their various kinds."

Genesis 1:11

So God created the great creatures of the sea and every living and moving thing with which the water teems, according to their kinds, and every winged bird according to its kind.

Genesis 1:21

And God said, "Let the land produce living creatures according to their kinds: livestock, creatures that move along the ground, and wild animals, each according to its kind."

Genesis 1:24

Do you see the special saying that is repeated again and again? God created different kinds of sea creatures, of birds and animals. And God said, "*Let each produce more of its own kind.*" The Hebrew word translated "kind" (*min*) is a general word. It does not fit any current term used by biologists. But in the Bible it refers to genus, family, order and species. And in Genesis *min* identifies the original genetic stock of plants and animals. All the plants and animals on Earth now have come from these original plants and animals.

There are different breeds of dogs, but dogs produce their own kind! A dog and a cat cannot mate and produce a new kind of animal. To mate, a pair must both be dogs, and their offspring will always be dogs—never cats.

Some scientists have made fun of the Bible and the word "kinds." But if we understand "kind" as plants or animals which contained the original code for the many breeds and varieties now on Earth, we can see just how trustworthy the Bible is. There is the kind of evolutionary change that Darwin noted so many years ago. But those variations were already built into the genes God gave the first plants or animals of that kind when he created all living things.

Just For Fun

1 Make a list of ways that you are different from your parents. List also how you are similar to them. Are the differences evolution (with a small "e") or Evolution (with a capital "E")?

2 How many different kinds of dogs can you identify? Do you suppose God created a single dog pair at first or several breeds?

3 Explain three ideas of how Evolution (with a capital "E") happened. What's wrong with each?

4 If you read in a high school biology book that the pepper moths of England "prove" the Theory of Evolution, what would you say?

5 If someone wants to know why you think Evolution cannot have happened in the plant or animal world, ask him to read *The Natural Limits to Biological Change*, by L. P. Lester and Raymond G. Bohlin (Grand Rapids, MI.: Zondervan) 1984.

9 THE RECORD IN THE ROCKS

The Theory of Evolution holds that one-celled creatures grew and changed into the many complex plants and animals we know today. But rocks contain the remains of plants and animals evolutionists believe are ancient. Do these remains, called fossils, really support the Theory of Evolution?

What is a fossil?

Fossils are hardened remains or traces of plants and animals that are found in the rocks of Earth's crust. Nearly all fossils are found in sedimentary rocks, which have been formed by flowing water.

Imprints of fish or plants found in rock are examples of fossils found in the rocks of Earth.

There are several different kinds of fossils. Some fossils are *petrified*. Petrified fossils have been turned to stone, as minerals fill up hollows in bones or wood. There are also *print fossils*, such as footprints left in mud that later turned into stone. *Mold fossils* are made when mud covers an organism. The plant or animal decays, but the mud around it turns into rock, leaving a hollow space. *Resin* fossils occur when an insect or spider is caught in tree sap, which later turns into amber. Sometimes in a resin fossil an insect may be preserved so well that scientists can count the hairs on its body. There are also unusual occurrences when a long-dead animal is preserved whole, like the frozen mammoth described on page 44. Fossils are important because they tell us what kind of plants and animals lived on the Earth long ago.

What do fossils have to do with the Theory of Evolution?

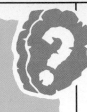

Evolutionists believe that life originated by chance, as single cells formed in shallow oceans (see chapter 7).

They also insist that those single cells somehow developed into more and more complex plants and animals. In fact, a person who holds the Theory of Evolution *must* argue that those first living cells changed. Some cells must have become bone cells, and others nerve cells and muscle cells. Some cells became the different kinds of cells in eyes, and others cells in teeth. Some cells became heart cells, and others became stomach cells. These cells are all very different, and no one can explain just how such changes could have taken place (see chapter 8). Yet evolutionists firmly believe that this unlikely kind of change took place.

What is important about fossils is that fossils are the only possible real evidence to which evolutionists can turn to support their theory. If living things did develop in the way Evolution proposes, becoming more and more complex, there should be fossil evidence! That is, the remains of long-dead plants and animals should include the slowly changing transition creatures, as fish turned into reptiles and reptiles into mammals.

Smaller changes should be recorded as well, as an ancestral fish turned into many kinds of fish, and as an ancestral bird turned into other kinds of birds. In fact, a complete fossil record would reveal an unbroken sequence of the gradual changes branching out from those original simple cells into all the complex and diverse creatures living in our world today.

Actually, evolutionists do propose an "evolutionary tree" (page 84). If evolutionists could actually take fossils from the earth, and lay them out in the pattern of this tree, showing how creatures developed step by step along the branches, they would have compelling evidence for their theory!

But while you can see diagrams of the supposed evolutionary tree in textbooks, you will *not* see actual fossils that show step-by-step changes. What does the fossil record show? Gaps! Different kinds of creatures simply appear in the rocks, without any evidence of step-by-step changes between them. Stephen Gould, one of today's leading evolutionists, wrote in 1980:

> The extreme rarity of transitional forms in the fossil record persists as the trade secret of paleontology. The evolutionary trees that adorn our textbooks have data only at the tips and nodes of their branches; the rest is inference, however reasonable, not the evidence of fossils. All paleontologists know that the fossil record contains precious little in the way of intermediate forms; transitions between major groups are characteristically abrupt.[1]

These gaps in the fossil record have become a real problem for anyone who holds to the Theory of Evolution.

What did Charles Darwin think about fossils?

Charles Darwin is the Englishman who, in the 1850s, argued for the Theory of Evolution. He wrote a famous book titled *On the Origin of the Species*. Many of Darwin's ideas are now questioned by scientists. But most still accept his notion that all life developed gradually from single cells.

Charles Darwin was troubled by the fossils that had been discovered in his time. In fact, one evolutionist reports that Darwin thought the fossil record was evidence *against* his Theory of Evolution because there were no fossils that showed one kind of creature turning into another.[2]

In 1859 Darwin himself wrote that the fossil record must be very poor, with many forms lost, because there simply were no fossils that showed changes between species. Darwin was surprised by the "sudden appearance" of whole groups of plant and animal fossils, and even decided that "those who believe the geological record is in any degree complete, will undoubtedly at once reject *my* theory."[3] Darwin did not doubt his Theory of Evolution. Instead he decided that people just hadn't found the *right* fossils. Somewhere, Darwin thought, there *must* be evidence of the kind of changes that his Theory of Evolution required.

It has been over one hundred years since Darwin wrote about the lack of fossil evidence for his theory. In 130 more years of searching, literally millions of fossils have been uncovered. Thousands of varieties of creatures have been identified, with thousands of branches to

People who believe the Theory of Evolution say that all living creatures developed from single-celled organisms into the many, widely varying forms of life we see today.

be accounted for on the evolutionary tree. *Yet there is not one complete sequence in the entire fossil record of change from one kind of plant or animal to another*! And this fact is admitted by modern scientists, like evolutionist Steven M. Stanley, who wrote in 1979 that "the known fossil record fails to document a single example of phyletic evolution accomplishing a major morphologic transition and hence offers no evidence that the gradualistic model can be valid."[4] If we translate the technical words, what Dr. Stanley says is simply this:

- There is not one complete fossil sequence of slow change from one kind of plant or animal to another!
- There is no evidence at all that a gradual change from simpler to more complex plants and animals actually took place!

If we look honestly at the fossil evidence, then, its weight is *against* Darwin's Theory of Evolution. If anything, the fossil evidence reveals that an evolutionary development of living creatures never took place!

Despite the evidence against the Theory of Evolution, evolutionists have not abandoned it. Instead they try to explain the failure of the fossil record to support their theory, and argue that what is found really does support Evolution anyway.

What are strata?

Nearly all fossils are found in sedimentary rocks. These are rocks formed by rapidly or slowly moving waters, which deposit sand and other minerals. The fossils we find in rocks were buried before the plant or animal could decay or be eaten.

"Stratum" is a word used to refer to a layer of rock thought to have been laid down in the same general period of time. There are many different strata, or layers, of sedimentary rock on Earth's crust. In some places, several miles of different layers of sedimentary rocks are found lying on top of one another.

Two kinds of scientists are very interested in rock strata. Geologists are scientists who study rocks and rock formations. Paleontologists are scientists who study the fossils found in rocks. What interests these scientists is that the same kinds of fossils are usually found in the same strata, and that certain kinds of fossils are usually (but not always!) found below or above other kinds of fossils.

These scientists have developed a theory presented in something called the "standard geologic column." They have arranged the different strata of rocks in order, from what they think are the oldest strata to the newest. The "standard geologic column" is made up of all the rock strata and is between 100 and 200 miles thick. At the bottom are rocks supposedly billions of years old, with "younger" rocks laid on top of them.

It is important to remember that the standard geologic column is theoretical. There is no place on Earth you can go to see the standard column. In fact, the average thickness of rock strata in any one place is only one mile, not 200! Yet even though there is no real geologic column that they can go to, geologists use the *idea* of a geologic column in their

THE GEOLOGIC COLUMN

EPOCH	BEGAN (MILLIONS OF YEARS AGO)	ASSUMED SEQUENCE OF BIOLOGICAL AND GEOLOGICAL EVENTS	IMPORTANT STATEMENTS BY EVOLUTIONISTS
Holocene	0.025	Modern man, plants, animals, warm climates	"The more one studies paleontology, the more certain one becomes that evolution is based on faith alone...."
Pleistocene	0.6-1	Modern species; giant mammals and many plants become extinct; man continues to develop; continents in high relief; cold and mild climates	"As yet we have not been able to trace the phylogenetic history of a single group of modern plants from its beginning to the present."

PERIOD Quaternary

EPOCH	BEGAN	EVENTS	STATEMENTS
Pliocene	12	Modern mammals; man emerges from apemen; modern invertebrates; continents elevated; dry, cool climate	"...there is still no general agreement as to where true *Homo sapiens*, the men of our own species, developed."
Miocene	25	Development of grazing mammals; first apemen; development of plains and grasslands; moderate climate	"One cannot assume that man is made-over anthropoid ape of any sort, for much of the available evidence is strongly against that assumption."
Oligocene	34	Primitive apes; whales; development of modern mammals; temperate plants; mountain building; mild climate	
Eocene	55	First horses; placental mammals; subtropical forests; North America and Europe connected; mountain erosion; heavy rains	"The real origin of horses is unknown."
Paleocene	75	Modern birds; dinosaurs extinct; placental mammals; subtropical plants; mountain building; temperate and subtropical climates	

PERIOD Tertiary

ENOZOIC ERA
(Age of Mammals)

EPOCH	BEGAN	EVENTS	STATEMENTS
	130	Extinction of giant reptiles; rise of pouched and placental mammals; flowering plants; spreading inland seas and swamps; mountain building; mild to cool climates	"... but I still think that to the unprejudiced, the fossil record of plants is in favor of special creation."

PERIOD Cretaceous

	180	Giant dinosaurs; first mammals; first toothed birds; shallow seas cover areas of continents; some mountain building	"Their [egg-laying mammals] geologic history is completely unknown."

PERIOD Jurassic

	230	First dinosaurs; dominant plants; continents rise; many deserts	Small insectivore types whose relationship to these reptiles is not at all clear

PERIOD Triassic

MESOZOIC ERA
(Age of Reptiles)

	260	Reptiles displace amphibians; extinction of many marine invertebrates; modern insects; evergreens arise; rise of continents; mountain building; some glaciation; cold climates	

PERIOD Permian

EPOCH	BEGAN (MILLIONS OF YEARS AGO)	ASSUMED SEQUENCE OF BIOLOGICAL AND GEOLOGICAL EVENTS	IMPORTANT STATEMENTS BY EVOLUTIONISTS
PERIOD Pennsylvanian	310	First reptiles; giant insects; shallow inland seas; some glaciation; swamp-forests; warm, moist climates	"There is no direct proof from the fossil record, but we can readily hypothesize the conditions under which [the origin of reptiles] came about."
PERIOD Mississippian	350	Amphibians spread; insects with wings; sharks and bony fish; inland seas; mountain building; hot swamplands; warm climates	
PERIOD Devonian **(Age of Fishes)**	400	First amphibians; freshwater fish; lungfish and sharks; forests and land plants; wingless insects; small inland seas; mountain building; heavy rains	"Just how fins developed into limbs is still a mystery—but they did."
PERIOD Silurian	425-430	Land invaded by anthropods and plants; continental seas cover flat continents; land rising; some mountain building; mild climates	"There is . . . no fossil evidence bearing on the question of insect origin."
PERIOD Ordovician **(Age of Invertebrates)**	475	First vertebrates (fish) appear; trilobites abundant; some land plants; lands submerge and oceans enlarge; warm, mild climates	"The best place to start the evolution of the vertebrates is in the imagination." "The geological record has so far provided no evidence as to the origin of fishes...."
PERIOD Cambrian	550	Marine invertebrates and algae; many invertebrates; trilobites are dominant; lowlands; mild climates	"The first and most important steps of animal evolution remain even more obscure than those of plant evolution."

PALEOZOIC ERA
(Age of Amphibians)

EPOCH	BEGAN	EVENTS	STATEMENTS
PERIOD Algonkian	2,000	Algae; sponges; marine worms; autotrophism established; volcanic activity; mountain building; glaciation; much erosion; warm climate	"We can . . . only speculate regarding their [the jellyfish] origin. . . ."
PERIOD Archean	4,000-4,500	Life first arose; heterotrophism established; lava flows; much sedimentation and erosion	"We do not know how life began." "If there has been evolution of life, the absence of the requisite fossils in the rocks older than the Cambrian is puzzling."

PRECAMBRIAN ERA

study of Earth's crust. And paleontologists use the column in their study of fossils.

In the standard geologic column, strata have been grouped by their supposed age. These groups of strata have been given names that represent the era in which they are thought to have been deposited. If you pick up a geology book, you'll read about Miocene, Jurassic and other rocks, named for the time period during which the rocks are thought to have formed.

The chart on pages 86 and 87 lists the names which scientists have given to different groups of strata. It tells when most geologists think the groups of strata were formed. The chart also lists the kinds of plants and animals that are found in these rock strata. If we look at the chart closely, we note that younger strata *do not have* many types of plants and animals that appear later.

This general correspondence between the plants and animals on the geologic column and the order in which evolutionists say they must have developed is often seen as positive proof of the Theory of Evolution. But in fact, it is evidence *against* the Theory of Evolution! Why?

First, the geologic column evolutionists use is complete. That is, there are no missing strata. Every stratum listed in the column has been found somewhere on Earth. Yet nowhere in any of these strata have fossils been found that show a step-by-step change from one kind of living creature to another! Again and again, as noted on the chart, evolutionists have been forced to admit that the kind of changes their theory

requires cannot be demonstrated from the fossil record.

Evolutionists still argue that the fossil record is incomplete. They say that when more fossils are found, the step-by-step changes their theory requires will be demonstrated. But everywhere, the record does show *the same systematic gaps* that troubled Darwin. Despite the millions of fossils found since his day, no step-by-step evidence has been produced!

Second, groups of plants and animals appear suddenly in the strata. In one age a particular kind of plant or animal is not there. In the next, suddenly and without stages of development, it *is* there. Regardless of how we might explain the appearance of new types of plants or animals in the geologic column, their

The rocks near Agate Springs, Nebraska contain bones of thousands of animals in pure limestone. They are jumbled together and could not have fallen into a sinkhole, as some evolutionists have claimed. Powerful, rushing water must have deposited them in this rock layer, which stretches for miles under the Nebraska prairie.

sudden appearance is strong evidence against a Theory of Evolution that depends on gradual change from one type of creature to another.

Third, the distinctive creatures that appear during a geologic age show *little or no change* over time. According to what is found in the geologic column, the different kinds of creatures either existed for many millions of years and then became extinct, as did the dinosaurs, or they are alive today! If the Theory of Evolution were correct, there should have been gradual evolutionary changes in creatures. What the fossil record shows, however, is *stasis*. Fossils show little or no change during the entire span of time a particular kind of creature existed.

So the argument for Evolution found in the arrangement of fossil creatures on the geologic column isn't that good after all. It's almost as if you were downtown and thought you recognized a friend across the street. You called out, dashed over to him, and then realized you'd made a mistake. When you got closer, you saw that he didn't even *look* like your friend. He was taller, had different color hair and had a much bigger nose.

It's something like this with the geologic column. At first glance you think it supports the Theory of Evolution. But when you get closer you realize that it does not. You see the gaps where step-by-step changes just don't exist in the fossil record. You see the sudden appearance of different kinds of creatures. And you note *stasis*, as all the kinds of creatures you discover simply do not change for what evolutionists say was mil-

lions of years. When you look closely, you realize that this doesn't even *look* like evidence for the Theory of Evolution. In fact, it looks like evidence against that theory!

Other problems, too

There are other problems for people who look at the fossil record to find evidence for the Theory of Evolution. So much of what is found just does not fit. Rock strata often do not fit together as they should. Sometimes "older" rocks are found on "younger" rocks, with no evidence they were jumbled or turned over. In some places rock strata will skip whole geologic eras, with rock supposedly millions of years younger laid directly on rock millions of years older, as though nothing had happened at that place for ages.

Fossils are also found out of order. In some places fossil trees extend through rock strata supposedly laid down millions of years apart.

One of many examples of fossil finds that do not fit the evolutionary theory is found in a great slab of sedimentary rock near Agate Springs, Nebraska. This slab holds the bones of some 9,000 different animals, all jumbled up together. These animals, which include rhinoceroses, camels, giant boars and many other strange as well as modern animals, were all tossed together by some violent flood and were buried quickly, before their bodies could decay or be eaten. The sudden burial together of kinds of animals who should not be found in the same part of the world is the kind of find that cannot be accounted for by the Theory of Evolution.

So the fossil record does not support the Theory of Evolution and is, in fact, filled with evidence against Evolution! Even when we examine the few fossils that evolutionists say *are* transition (change) forms, we find the evidence for Evolution is terribly weak.

Taking wings

Two years after Darwin's book *On the Origin of the Species* was published, a beautifully preserved fossil creature was discovered. This strange creature had features of both a bird and a reptile, and was given the name *Archeopteryx* (ancient bird). Evolutionists still claim that Archeopteryx is a "missing link" in the transition from reptiles to birds. The book *Life on Earth* (1980) says "Even today, there is no more convincing example of such a link."

The "reptilelike" features of Archeopteryx are clawlike growths on the front edge of its wings, a jaw with teeth rather than a beak, and a backbone that extends out along its tail. Archeopteryx also lacked the "deep-keeled" breastbone where muscles needed for flight are attached in birds. It also had a short wingspan.

Even so, Archeopteryx was definitely a bird. It had a birdlike skull, wings, a wishbone, and it also had perfectly formed feathers. Wishbones are found only in birds, and feathers are their most distinctive features.

Some evolutionists argued that Archeopteryx could not use its wings to fly, but instead ran along the ground and used its wings to swat bugs! But the evidence is that Archeopteryx could fly. In fact the wing feathers of Archeopteryx are designed for rapid flight, like those of swifts and falcons. So Archeopteryx could not only glide but could actively flap along, although perhaps not as well as some modern birds.

One thing Archeopteryx probably could not do was take off from the ground. Its small breastbone would not have supported muscles needed for it to launch itself. It probably leaped into the air from a tree branch. Quite possibly the sharp, hooked claws on its wing were for grasping the trunk of a tree as it struggled up for another launch. Actually, some birds today have "un-birdlike" claws they use for climbing. Among them are the South American hoatzin and the African turaco.

But what about Archeopteryx as a transition form, or missing link, between reptiles and birds? While Archeopteryx is unusual, it is very poor evidence for such a transition. *All the really important features of birds are present in Archeopteryx and are fully formed!* A true transition form, one which showed evidence of a step-by-step change, should have some major features of the "new" creature, and at least a few of those features should be only partially formed.

To say that a bird has reptilelike features is *not* proof that it is a transition form between reptiles and birds. If evolutionists are to present solid evidence for evolutionary change, they need to find fossils that show a *sequence of changes* rather than an isolated creature like Archeopteryx with "reptilelike" features.

Evidence is for creation

In these last few chapters we've looked at critical issues for the Theory of Evolution. That theory asserts that life began by change from combinations of non-living chemicals. Yet we saw in chapter seven that it could not possibly have begun in that way. The Theory of Evolution asserts that all living creatures developed from original one-celled beings, which became more and more complex. Yet we saw in chapter eight that the scientific evidence is *against* every possible mechanism evolutionists have suggested to explain how such changes could take place. In this chapter we've looked at the fossil record to see whether or not there is evidence of the kind of change in plants and animals that there *must* be if the Theory of Evolution is correct. And again we've seen that the evidence is against, not for, that theory.

If we consider the scientific evidence, then, the weight of that evidence is definitely for creation and not for the Theory of Evolution. And, as we will see in the next section, even stronger evidence for creation can be found by examining the creatures that are living today.

Just For Fun

1 Use your imagination. Draw a fish. Then draw several pictures to show how that fish might turn into a bird or a horse. Do you think something like that could actually happen? Why, or why not?

2 Are there any hills in your area where you can see strata of sedimentary rocks? If there are, go on a fossil hunt! Take a small hammer and carefully chip away at the rock.

3 Explain to someone why the fossil record is evidence against the Theory of Evolution.

4 Look at the chart on pages 86 and 87, and read the quotes of scientists who believe in Evolution but admit there are no transition forms. Why do you suppose they continue to hold the Theory of Evolution?

5 Some Christians think that God first created simple kinds of plants and animals and then waited millions of years to create other, more complicated kinds. What do you think about this idea?

EVIDENCE FROM LIVING THINGS

And God said, "Let the land produce living creatures according to their kinds..."

10 THE SAME, YET DIFFERENT

Evolutionists have long pointed to similarities between different kinds of animals as evidence for the Theory of Evolution. But are similarities really good evidence? In this chapter we find out. And in the next three chapters we look at amazing facts about living animals that the Theory of Evolution simply *cannot* explain!

For many years the horse was considered positive proof of the Theory of Evolution. The 1969 Time-Life book *Evolution* (p. 112) made this claim:

The development of the modern horse has been traced back some 60 million years from the tall, graceful animal of today to a short-necked creature not much larger than a domestic cat. Originally the horse was a forest dweller with many toes, well adapted to travel on the soft, moist earth of tropical North America. As the climate grew colder and the forest thinned into an open grassy plain, the horse slowly developed hard, single toes for traveling on dry land, and complicated grinding teeth for feeding on the scanty herbage of the Great Plateau.[1]

College students just twenty-five years ago were shown pictures of animals and fossils like those in the pictures on page 95. They were told that the evolution of the horse was a fact and that all intelligent people *must* believe in Evolution.

Today *no evolutionist thinks that the "short-necked creature not much bigger than a domestic cat" is related*

Could a racehorse have evolved from a creature the size of a housecat? For decades evolutionists insisted yes. But no longer!

to the modern horse at all. The fossil called Eohippus, or Dawn Horse, is now considered to be a close relative of the rock rabbit!

Why do paleobiologists no longer believe in the "evolutionary history" of the horse? One reason is that fossil bones of horses have been found in the same rock strata where the Dawn Horse was found. These horses were the ancestors of the modern horse!

There are other reasons, too. The fossils that evolutionists linked in their series actually came from all over the world, not just America. As for size, some modern horses (like Shetland ponies) are no larger than the smaller "horses" found in the fossil record.

But *why* did evolutionists ever think fossils from different parts of the world should be linked together in the first place? Part of the reason is that they were tricked by their own theory. The Theory of Evolution said that modern animals should develop from similar but different animals of the past. It said that hooves should be an adaptation and have developed from several toes to one. Size would help a horse survive by enabling it to run faster, so animals should gradually become larger. Simply put, evolutionists fit the fossil bones of different animals into a series and said they were horses, because the bones fit their Theory of Evolution!

It's almost as if you were outside one day and found a tennis ball, a soccer ball and a basketball in a weedy field. You noticed that each ball is hollow, and each has an increasingly thicker skin. You're really

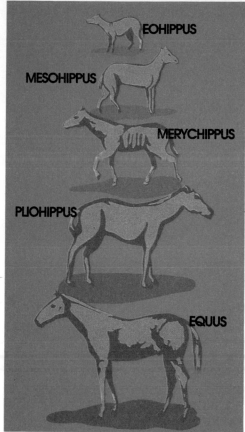

Textbooks and museums once showed these pictures of "ancestors of the modern horse," which they claimed proved the Theory of Evolution. Today no one believes that the horse developed this way.

excited, and figure that each evolved from some common ancestor! Then you spend the rest of your life trying to figure out *how* that could possibly have happened. You invent story after story to explain that evolution, and even though the evidence is against each suggestion you make, many people believe you. They don't seem to realize that finding the balls lined up in a particular order doesn't prove descent at all.

But when evolutionists arrange fossil sequences, like that of the supposed horse ancestors, they go even further. They *use their theory to arrange the bones.* Since evolutionists used their theory to arrange the bones of the supposed ancestors of the horse, no one should *ever* have assumed the arrangement proved the theory. Yet they assumed just that, until more evidence forced them to admit they were wrong!

Is similarity proof?

Evolutionists were not trying to trick people when they said they had traced the ancestry of the horse. In fact, they tricked themselves! So we need to ask an important question. *Why* did they think the fossil remains traced the evolution of the horse? The answer is that each fossil

skeleton was similar in many ways to the others and similar to the skeleton of the modern horse.

In biology there is a special name for similarities in the way animal parts are structured. When, for example, the front leg or arm bones of animals are similar, they are said to be *homologous.* For many years evolutionists have claimed that *homology* is strong evidence for their theory.

There *are* many similarities between animals, and between animals and human beings. If you examine the head of a horse, you find muscles that are used for moving the ears and wrinkling the forehead. Very similar muscles are found in the head of a person! Animals that run on four legs have a very similar design. Apes and monkeys have a design that is very similar to human beings.

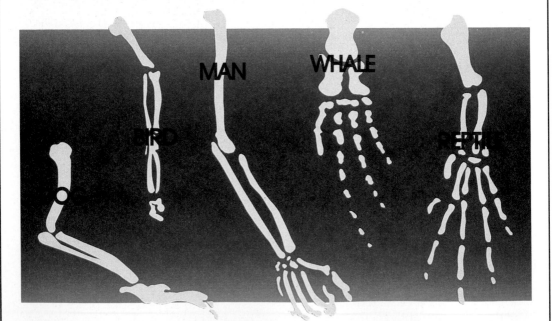

MAN

WHALE

BIRD

REPTILE

The front limbs of these mammals are homologous (similar). Can you find similarities and differences? Some people claim that such similarities are evidence for the Theory of Evolution. But is this really a good argument?

What is more, the nerves of animals, the blood circulation systems, the ability to see and taste and smell, all show a similar design.

According to many people, such similarities are evidence for the Theory of Evolution and can only be explained if animal kinds grew out of one another or if all share a common ancestor.

It was the idea that *homology (similarity) proves relationship* that led scientists to believe in the supposed evolutionary history of the horse. The fossil bones *were* similar. And they fit the idea of what the evolutionists thought *should* have happened. So for many years evolutionists were sure that the horse *did* evolve the way they said it had.

But they were wrong. Somehow, homology was not such good evidence for the Theory of Evolution after all!

Why is homology not good evidence?

The first thing wrong with homology as a proof of Evolution is the notion that Evolution is the only explanation for similarities. If Evolution were the only possible explanation for similarities, it might be a good argument. But the person who believes God created living creatures has another explanation to offer.

What is the explanation? Simply that God developed a basic plan and used this plan in creating living things. There are many reasons to think this is the best possible explanation for homology.

Think, for instance, about There are many different kind houses. Some are mansions wi many rooms. Others are small a inexpensive. Some have two stories, others only one floor. Some have basements, and others are built on cement slabs. Some houses have many windows, and some only a few. But despite these differences, houses share a similar basic plan. Nearly all have kitchens, living rooms, bathrooms and bedrooms. They have heating systems, roofs, doors and windows.

Now clearly all these similarities do not mean that houses evolved from some common ancestor. The similarities show that houses were designed to meet the same basic needs. Houses have kitchens because everyone needs to prepare food. They have bedrooms because people need a place to sleep. They have roofs to keep out the rain, and doors so people can go in and out. What do these similarities prove? Why, they prove that houses have been intelligently planned in order to meet common needs!

If you think about it for a minute, you'll see homology in the animal world is evidence for the very same thing. Similarities are evidence that God, an intelligent being, has consciously designed animals to meet common needs!

For an animal to live in the world God created, there are certain things it must be able to do. It must eat, breathe, move, reproduce, and so on. In order to eat, an animal needs a mouth. It needs a jaw and teeth to chew food, a stomach and intestines to digest it, and a way to pass waste materials out of the body.

An animal needs a nose to breathe in air. It needs lungs to take the oxygen out of the air and a blood system to carry oxygen and food to the different cells of its body. An animal needs a heart to pump blood through the blood vessels that go throughout the body.

To be aware of the world around it, an animal needs senses—sight, hearing, taste and smell. An animal needs nerves to carry sensations, and a brain to interpret the messages its nerves carry. And an animal needs limbs to carry it from place to place.

Now all these are basic needs of living creatures. So when God created living creatures, he developed a common design to meet them, just as architects use a common design when planning a house!

Yet there are many amazing *variations* on the basic plan God used in designing living creatures. And it's far more difficult for the evolutionist to explain the variations than it is for a creationist to explain the similarities. We'll look at some of the variations in the next chapters. But we should not be surprised if God's basic design remains pretty much the same.

Yet the similarities are not all that surprising. Homology is to be expected. The similarities are not evidence for the Theory of Evolution at all. Similarities demonstrate God's skill as the great Designer and Giver of life!

What are problems with homology?

When evolutionists mistakenly arranged the supposed fossil ancestors of the horse, they looked only at the bones. The bone structure was similar, and they supposed that the structural homology meant common ancestry.

But what would they have thought if they looked at the shape of a dolphin or whale, and compared them to the shape of a fish? The shapes are homologous. Each has fins rather than legs. Each is clearly designed to live in the water. If homology proves Evolution, then modern fish and dolphins might be expected to have the same ancestor.

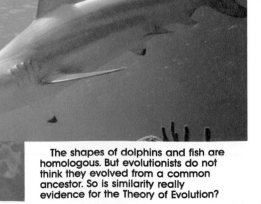

The shapes of dolphins and fish are homologous. But evolutionists do not think they evolved from a common ancestor. So is similarity really evidence for the Theory of Evolution?

But there is a problem here. Fish are cold-blooded creatures. They lay eggs and breathe by gills that take oxygen from the water. Dolphins are mammals. They give birth to live young. They are warm-blooded. And they have lungs, not gills, and breathe air. If we ignore the similarity of shape and look at other structures, dolphins would not have evolved from fish but from land animals!

Evolutionists can't explain the homologous shape of sea mammals and fish by saying that they evolved from a common ancestor. No evolutionist thinks for a moment that they did! So perhaps homologous structures shouldn't be used as evidence for Evolution at all!

The fact is that in the animal and insect world there are dozens of animals that look quite similar, but whose softer tissues and organs prove they *cannot* be related at all.

Similarity of function is actually a problem for the Theory of Evolution. For instance, flying demands amazingly complex and specialized structures and instinctual skills. Yet such diverse creatures as birds, bats and many insects all fly. Evolutionists have not been able to explain the evolution of flight or even guess how it could occur. What's more, this complex ability is found over and over in the animal world where *there is no evolutionary connection possible between the flying creatures*!

Simply put, homologous appearance is more of a *problem* for the Theory of Evolution than a proof of it! Homology is much better evidence of a Designer who used a similar plan to construct very different kinds of animal life.

What about other similarities?

Evolutionists still organize animals into families by homologous structures and argue that similarities are a major proof for their Theory of Evolution. And they have also looked for other kinds of similarity. Some have turned to blood tests to try to "prove" evolutionary descent. These tests are designed to show how closely the blood of different species resembles human blood.

In 1902 when the English evolutionist Nuttall conducted his first tests, he discovered that the more like a human being an animal species appears to be, the more white flakes the test produces in the animal's blood. He found no flakes produced in the blood of reptiles. Some was produced in the blood of animals like horses. And more was produced in the blood of monkeys. The most flakes were produced in the blood of the great apes.

Nuttall argued that the similarity of blood proved the Theory of Evolution. But why stop with blood? Why not look at other similarities on a chemical level? If we do look beyond blood, we make some interesting discoveries. For instance, the active chemical produced by the thyroid gland is exactly the same in a sheep and a human being. Does that mean sheep are ancestors of humans?

Recently scientists have been able to analyze the amino acids in animal proteins. One important protein in animals is cytochrome c. It is often used as evidence for the Theory of

Evolution, since unlike other proteins, it fits fairly closely to evolutionists' notions of evolutionary descent. Yet when cytochrome c differences are analyzed, what do we find? On the basis of this similarity, rattlesnakes are more closely related to human beings than to another reptile, the snapping turtle! Human beings are closer to the Peking duck than to another mammal, the horse!

Hemoglobin is the protein that carries oxygen in red blood cells. It is one of the most complex of molecules, having an eight-helix folded pattern. Hemoglobin occurs in most vertebrates, but also in earthworms, clams, some insects and some bacteria. In each, the complex molecule is exactly the same. But as far as Evolution is concerned, there is *no common line of descent for the creatures that have hemoglobin.* And it is impossible to imagine that the entire eight-helix folded pattern in the hemoglobin molecule could develop by chance in such different creatures.

What does the evidence show?

Those who believe in the Theory of Evolution like to say that homology is evidence for their favorite theory. But as we've seen, the evidence is not all that convincing.

The shapes of fish and dolphins are similar—but their internal structures are very different. Creatures who have no possible evolutionary connection can fly or have similarities like the amazing hemoglobin molecule. The broken pattern of similarities and differences is much better evidence for the existence of a Designer who created living things than it is for the Theory of Evolution which denies him. God has filled this world with many beauties and wonders, including living things that are strikingly different.

But the evidence still does not convince the evolutionist who wants to explain all things without God. Michael Land, a scientist who studied tiny shrimplike animals that live deep in the ocean, illustrates. These similar animals were found to have compound eyes with many different facets. Yet some of the animals have "lens cylinders" that bend the lights, where others have a mirrorlike system that reflects light to a single point. These different eye systems are so complex that Land could not imagine a common ancestor. He concluded that they could not be evolutionary relatives, even though in every other way they seemed the same. In fact, Land says that while studying "the marvelous design of" the eyes, he was trying not to conclude that "these eyes had been put there by God to confuse scientists."[2] It is not that God has failed to fill this universe with abundant evidence of his presence. It's simply that those who are committed to the Theory of Evolution will not consider the possibility of creation, however compelling the evidence may be.

Just For Fun

1 In a college zoology course (zoology is the study of animals), these two test questions were on the final exam: "Did you believe in Evolution when you started this course?" and "Do you believe in Evolution now?" Why do you think these questions were on the test? How would you have answered the questions?

2 In some natural history museums you can still see a "picture history" of the "evolution" of the horse, like the picture series on page 95. Visit a museum and find displays that are supposed to prove the Theory of Evolution. Now that you have read this far, can you see what is wrong with that evidence?

3 Look at pictures of four different animals. List ways they are similar and ways they are different. How might an evolutionist explain the similarities? How could you explain them?

4 Evolutionists believe that human beings and apes are closely related. What do you think are the most important *differences* between apes and people? How do you think evolutionists might explain these differences?

5 While many things about animals are similar, there are also unique things that make kinds of animals special. What is your favorite kind of animal? What makes that kind of animal special and different from others?

11 THE WONDERS OF DESIGN

The animal world is full of wonders. As we look at some of the animals which share our Earth, the things we discover make the Theory of Evolution less and less believable. So many features of living things give clear evidence of careful, matchless design that we simply must believe in a Designer.

Imagine driving with your family in Yellowstone National Park. You drive slowly, looking at the mountains and pointing out the different animals you see. Then your dad pulls over to the side of the road! There's one of the park's major attractions: the bears!

They come near your car, and your dad pushes the control button and raises your windows. The curious bears come right up to your car. One puts his forepaws on the side of the car, presses his nose against the window and peers right in at you!

Later, as you drive on, you talk excitedly about the bears. Of course, you don't say much about your car. I mean, after all, cars are just cars.

The fact is, however, both the bear and your car are wonders. That car you drive has a complicated engine that mixes gasoline and air. The gas and air mixture is exploded by a spark that flashes at just the right

time, and the energy of that explosion is transferred through the transmission to turn your car's wheels. The car has air-conditioning, so even when it's hot outside, it's cool inside. It has a radio, capable of receiving

Both the bears we watch and the cars we drive are wonders that demonstrate the principle of design.

signals sent through the air and re-producing them as music or speech.

No one looking carefully at your car and the complicated systems we take for granted would ever imagine that it had "just happened." There's too much evidence of planning and design. The elements of each system work together in ways that are far too complicated to have happened by chance.

Moreover, if we look closely at our bear or at other animals, we find something very similar. There are a variety of systems built into living creatures, too. These living systems have elements that are far too com-plicated to have happened by chance. Like that familiar car, whose design shows the touch of an intelli-gent maker, so are the systems built into living creatures also wonders of design. They too show the touch of an intelligent maker, God.

The woodpecker

One of the common birds that you may have seen is the woodpecker. You've seen him gripping the trunk of a tree, pounding away with his beak. How can this bird hold onto the tree trunk, while other birds must perch on a branch? And how can this bird pound its beak against a tree again and again without at least getting a headache?

When we look closely, we find that there are many systems found only in the woodpecker that make him a most unusual bird. The feet of wood-peckers are not like the feet of other birds. Woodpeckers have two toes pointing backward and two forward, to hook into a tree trunk. Their tail feathers are short and stiff, so the

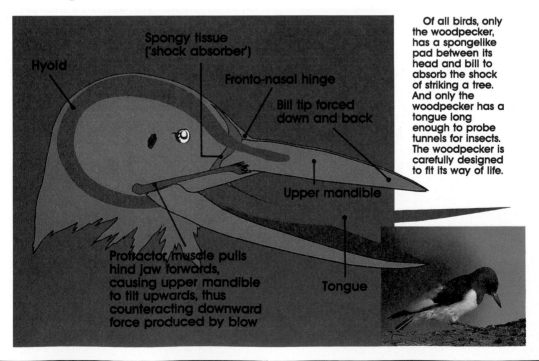

Hyoid

Spongy tissue ('shock absorber')

Fronto-nasal hinge

Bill tip forced down and back

Upper mandible

Protractor muscle pulls hind jaw forwards, causing upper mandible to tilt upwards, thus counteracting downward force produced by blow

Tongue

Of all birds, only the woodpecker, has a spongelike pad between its head and bill to absorb the shock of striking a tree. And only the woodpecker has a tongue long enough to probe tunnels for insects. The woodpecker is carefully designed to fit its way of life.

woodpecker can prop itself against the trunk.

But two things are most amazing about the woodpecker. First, just behind its pointed bill is a pad of spongy tissue that acts as a shock absorber. In other birds, the skull and bill are fused together. But because of this built-in shock absorber, far better than anything developed by man, woodpeckers can pound on hard wood for five or six hours a day. Some great spotted woodpeckers have actually pounded their way into "woodpecker proof" *concrete* boxes!

The woodpecker drills holes in order to reach wood-boring insects. But the bird seldom drills right to its prey. Instead it reaches one of the tunnels the insect has made within the wood. How can it reach the insect? Well, the woodpecker has an amazing tongue. The tongue is often longer than the bird. It is not attached to the back of the mouth, as are other birds' tongues, but circles around inside the skull to attach to the top of the woodpecker's head! Without a long tongue to probe insect tunnels, the woodpecker could not survive.

Every one of these special features—the unusual arrangement of the woodpecker's toes, the stiff and stubby tail, the shock absorber behind the bill, and the long tongue that lets it probe tunnels for insects—sets the woodpecker apart from other birds.

Yet each feature fits together to enable the woodpecker to live his specialized life. If any of these features were different, the woodpecker could not survive! Yet the Theory of Evolution would require each of

these special systems to have just happened and to have developed by chance at the same time! How much more reasonable to see in the woodpecker's special design the mind of God, who created the woodpecker for his unusual life.

The amazing penguin

Another example of a complicated and amazing design is seen in the penguin. This bird's "wings" are short flippers, designed for swimming through the water. Its feet, used for steering, are at the very end of the penguin's body, not under the middle as in other birds. Penguins also have unusual feathers. These are long and thin, but with fluffy tufts at their base. The tufts form a mat that wind and water cannot penetrate. This coat of feathers covers more of the bird's body than do the

Evolutionists do not explain the design of the penguin—or the amazing way the emperor penguins tend their chicks.

feathers of other birds. Also, under the feather coat penguins alone have a layer of blubber, or thick fat. Penguins are so well protected that instead of suffering from the cold of the Antarctic, they are in more danger of overheating!

But one of the most amazing things about penguins is the breeding pattern of the emperor penguin. This large bird spends the summer at sea, feeding. In March adults come ashore on sea ice and walk as far as ninety miles to their breeding grounds. For two months they search for a mate and wait until the female has laid her single, very large egg.

These birds lay eggs on ice because there is no material there from which to make nests. How can the penguin keep its egg from freezing?

Well, the emperor penguin has a fold of feathered skin hanging down from its belly. The female rolls the egg up onto her feet, and then covers it with that fold of skin. Immediately the male comes to the female and takes the egg onto his feet, hiding it beneath his fold of feathered skin.

The female then leaves, hurrying back to the water. There she feeds for nearly two months, while the male penguin just stands, waiting for that egg balanced on his feet to hatch.

And just when the egg does hatch, the female returns. She is just in time. She picks out her own mate and chick from the hundreds of thousands of penguins standing on the ice, and feeds the chick half-digested fish. This feeding literally saves his life. If the female were only a day or so late, the chick would die!

Now the male is free to hurry to sea. He gorges there for two weeks.

But then he too returns to his chick. Now it is the father's turn to arrive just in time. Although thousands of chicks now stand together, the male penguin recognizes his offspring and feeds it from the fish stored in his crop and stomach.

For the rest of the winter, the parents take turns going off to fish and bringing back food for their youngster. If at any time a parent were a day or so late, the chick would die.

What an amazing design! Each bird has an apron of feathered skin to warm the egg. Each takes its turn, standing with its back to blizzards and sleet. And each takes its turn traveling to the sea and back with food—always arriving just in time to feed the chick before it starves!

Patterns like this, which occur again and again in the animal world, are evidence of careful planning and design. How hard it is to imagine that the Theory of Evolution can offer a reasonable explanation for such complex patterns of behavior; how easy to see the hand of God!

The temperature bird

Doctors once had to feel the forehead or body of a sick person and guess at his temperature. Then someone invented the thermometer. But there is a bird with a built-in thermometer that is far more sensitive than the one in your home's medicine cabinet.

When the mallee fowl of Australia nests, it digs a great pit. It fills the pit with decaying leaves and piles sand on top of them. Then the female digs a tunnel in this material and lays her eggs. The eggs are kept warm by the heat produced by the decaying leaves!

But the bird does not leave her eggs. Instead she stays near her nest and, several times a day, pokes her beak into the sand. She does this to test the heat in the nest. Her tongue is such a good thermometer that she can tell a change of as little as 1/10 of a degree.

If the sand is too cool, the mother bird piles on more sand. If it is too hot, she scrapes sand away. Finally, after a very long time, the young mallee birds hatch and dig their way up out of the mound.

How can the bird tell just what temperature the eggs need? How did she know how to build her unusual nest? How does it happen that her tongue is a sensitive thermometer? Even if mutation and natural selection could account for this bird's tongue, how could chance mutations "teach" a bird to use its tongue in such a way or to build a nest of decaying leaves?

The first zipper

Actually, we don't have to go to unusual birds to find amazing design features. All birds are amazing— from the hollow bones that make them lighter and enable them to fly more easily to the pattern of their feathers.

In fact, it is hard to believe that *feathers* could just happen. Each feather is a marvel of engineering de-

sign. Barbs extend from each side of a center shaft. Smaller *barbules* grow out of both sides of the barbs, and these have tiny, microscopic *barbicels*. These barbicels are tiny hooks, and some birds have over a million barbicels on a single feather! The hooks fit into the next feather's barbules, weaving the whole together. And if the barbs are pulled apart, the bird hooks them back together by running its beak through the feathers!

Thus bird feathers not only have the world's first zippers built in, but the whole complex design is necessary to enable the wing to flare and hold air as it flies. The idea that this specialized, complicated structure somehow just happened to evolve from reptile scales is very strange if not ridiculous.

Directional signals?

Modern airplanes navigate electronically. They pick up radio signals or satellite signals, and complicated equipment translates the signals to tell the pilot his or her location. But for years we have known that birds can navigate across great distances without any such mechanical aids.

In one test of this incredible ability, a number of Manx shearwaters, which nest off the coast of Wales, were tagged and released at different points far beyond their usual range. One was turned loose in Boston, some 3,200 miles from home.

In just twelve and a half days the bird returned to its nest, having traveled about 250 miles a day, starting from a place thousands of miles from where it had ever been before. What's more, based on the known speed of the bird, it must have flown *directly* home, across the open ocean. How? No one knows. But the navigation system of this and other birds seems better than any mechanical system human beings have ever developed!

The first sonar?

Two modern scientific wonders are radar and sonar. Radar tells the location of objects that cannot be seen by bouncing radio waves off them. Sonar uses sound, measuring distance by the echoing "ping" of sound waves. Sonar was developed for underwater use in finding enemy submarines during World War II.

But from the beginning, bats have found their way by airborne sonar! Bats fly at night. Rather than rely on sight to locate the tiny insects they

Millions of bats fly out of a cave. Their amazing sonar keeps them from colliding with each other and lets them track the tiniest insect in flight.

eat, bats have a very sophisticated sonar system. They use sounds humans cannot hear, which vibrate between 50,000 and 200,000 times a second. The bat sends out these sounds in short clicks, making twenty or thirty each second. The bat's hearing is so sensitive that from the echo of each sound the bat can tell exactly where trees and other obstacles are. It can also tell the location of the tiniest flying insects.

During the day millions of bats sleep in many of the large caves in our Southwest. If you go into such a cave during the day and shine a bright light there, the air will suddenly be filled with hundreds of thousands of frightened, swirling bats. But no one bat will strike you. And not one bat will strike another, even though the air is filled with them!

How can the bats, terrified and flying packed together in a tightly enclosed space, keep from striking each other or the walls or you? Why don't they become mixed up as hundreds of thousands of sonar signals all sound at the same time? No one can tell! The perfection of the bat's sonar system is beyond our capacity to understand, but not beyond the capacity of our God to provide.

The first kite?

It's fun to make a kite, attach the tail, and launch it in a brisk breeze. But human beings did not invent kites.

Perhaps the first kite was flown by young spiders. Many of them, when they come out of their cocoons, climb to the top of a blade of grass and face the wind. They lift up their backs, and spin a tiny silken thread. This thread is drawn out by the slightest breeze. As the thread grows, the wind pulls on it. The baby spider clings to the grass until the thread is long enough, and then suddenly lets go—to sail off into the air!

When the spider lands in a new territory, it spins its web and begins its new life. But flying can be dangerous for spiders. Some have landed on ships hundreds of miles from shore, carried there on their silky kites.

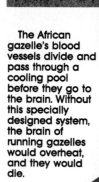

An unusual cooling system?

That car we talked about at the beginning of this chapter has a cooling system. Water or coolant circulates through the engine. It is carried to the radiator, where moving air cools it before it is circulated back through the engine. If there were no way to cool the engine, it would overheat and break down.

But human engineers did not invent the first cooling system. Every living warm-blooded creature has many mechanisms for temperature control. The fast-running gazelle of Africa must often sprint to escape its enemies. This sprint raises the temperature of the gazelle's body. But for the gazelle to survive, its brain must be kept cooler than the body.

To keep the brain cool the

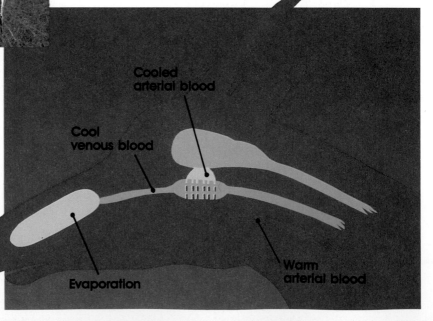

The African gazelle's blood vessels divide and pass through a cooling pool before they go to the brain. Without this specially designed system, the brain of running gazelles would overheat, and they would die.

Cooled arterial blood

Cool venous blood

Evaporation

Warm arterial blood

gazelle has its own cooling system, built right into its head. Gazelles and similar animals have hundreds of small arteries that divide and pass through a large pool of blood lying next to its breathing passages. The air that is inhaled cools this nasal pool, so the blood passing through the tiny arteries in it is cooled, too. Then the tiny arteries come together in a single blood vessel that carries blood to the brain.

Does this system work? Temperature differences have been measured in one small gazelle, which ran for five minutes at twenty-five miles an hour. The body temperature went up from 82°F to 93°F! But the temperature of the brain never even reached 86°F, which is safe for this animal.

Without its system for brain cooling, the gazelle simply could not survive.

There are many more examples of engineering design in the animal world. As we learn more about them, each discovery helps us be more comfortable about our faith. Are we foolish to believe in God? Hardly! It seems much more foolish to think that such marvels—on which the very lives of the animals involved hinge—could "just happen" by an Evolution whose processes cannot really be explained by even one evolutionist.

Just For Fun

1 Look back over the animals and birds described in this chapter. Which seem to have built-in clocks? Maps?

2 Which animal's or bird's design seems most complicated? Why?

3 Which animal's or bird's behavior seems most difficult to explain by the Theory of Evolution? Why?

4 How many different modern inventions (like water cooling an engine) can you find already operating in the birds and animals described in this chapter?

5 What other wonder in the animal world suggests that there must be a Creator who designed it?

12 MORE WONDERS OF DESIGN

The wonders of God's design are shown in more than physical structures. Design is also shown in patterns built into animal communities. These patterns are not learned, but deeply implanted, and are controlled by factors that even now can hardly be understood. As we look at them, we realize again that there is no way these things could have just happened.

Today we live in a world of mechanical wonders. Human beings have discovered and applied many fascinating principles—that are already built into God's animal creation.

We read about heat-seeking missiles that jet fighters can fire at each other. These missiles are so sensitive to heat that they home in on the exhaust of the enemy jet. The missiles follow that heat trail and destroy the enemy.

But did you know that rattlesnakes hunt at night using a similar sense? This sense is found in a cavity between the nostril and the eye, and it is so sensitive to heat that it can detect a rise of 3/100 of a degree! This sense enables the snake not only to tell if an animal is near, but it also tells the exact distance and direction, thus guiding its strike.

If you're a fishing enthusiast, you know all about lures. You can go into a sporting goods store and see many different artificial baits designed to fool fish into striking. When fish do strike,

The alligator snapper fishes in the same way we do—with an artificial lure.

110

they're caught by the hooks on the lure, and you reel them in!

But did you know that the alligator snapping turtle had the idea first? This turtle has a bright, red worm-like growth on the inside of its lower jaw. The turtle lies on the bottom of a pond with its mouth open, wiggling its little red bait. When a curious or hungry fish comes to look, the turtle closes its jaw—and gulps.

More examples of design

Everywhere we look on our Earth we find more wonders in the animal world. For instance, one bright, tiny jungle frog lays its eggs on a leaf. When the tadpoles hatch, the female frog lets one at a time wriggle up onto her back. She then finds a bromeliad leaf, which is shaped so that water collects in it. She carefully examines such a tiny pool, and if there is no sign of life she backs into it. The tadpole swims off. There, in its own private aquarium, the tadpole will live on eggs laid by insects in the pool.

One species of tree frog is even more involved. Every week the female visits the pools where her young are growing. She then lays an unfertilized egg (from which no tadpole could hatch) in the water. The tadpole lives on these eggs for the six or eight weeks it takes to turn into a frog.

If we look in the sea, we find more wonders. The largest living animal on Earth is the blue whale. It can weigh as much as twenty-five elephants! Yet it is one of a group called baleen whales, which have no teeth at all.

Instead of teeth, these whales have baleen, which are like curtains of horn that hang down from the roofs of their mouths. The only thing these giant whales eat is krill, which are tiny, shrimplike animals that swarm in the sea.

How do baleen whales eat this one item on their diet? Whales rush through the schools of krill, sucking in great mouthfuls of water. Then, with their tongues, they push the water out, half closing their mouths. The krill are caught on curtains of baleen and swallowed.

If the krill are not thick in a particular area, the whale may dive deep. Then it will spiral upward, forcing the krill toward the center of the spiral. When the tiny animals are thus concentrated in one place, the whale opens its mouth and sucks them in.

It is hard to imagine how the Theory of Evolution could explain the baleen that allows whales to feed on krill and krill alone. How much more likely that God designed the whale and the krill on which it feeds.

A termite's home is its castle

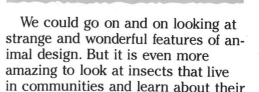

We could go on and on looking at strange and wonderful features of animal design. But it is even more amazing to look at insects that live in communities and learn about their behavior.

How do millions of tiny, blind insects build castle mounds that are wonders of design? Evolutionists do not explain the instincts that make such community projects possible.

For example, most termites are tiny insects with whitish, soft bodies. They must have a dark, moist place to live. Some termites placed in the open air will die within a few hours.

There are many termite groups that build different kinds of mounds. The *Macrotermes* of Africa build great castlelike mounds in which as

many as several million termites can be secure. Inside such mounds are "gardens" where the termites grow fungus for food.

Inside these castle mounds are many other wonders. Termites must have fresh, moist air. So their mounds are built with complicated ventilation systems. Air is heated by the bodies of the termites and their fungus. This warmed air rises, and tiny tunnels carry the rising warm air close to the surface of the mound. The tiny capillary tunnels are so near the porous surface that oxygen can actually be infused into the inside air and carbon dioxide can diffuse out. Cooled and refreshed, the air drops down through other tunnels to circulate all over again. Thus the castle mound actually acts like a giant lung and constantly refreshes the air inside it.

This air-moving system is so effective that the temperature inside the termite mound is kept at a steady 64 °F all year—no matter what the temperature is outside. And the moisture needed by the insects is constantly circulated through the whole mound.

But how are these marvelous castles, with their complicated air-circulation and temperature-control tunnels, made? Each huge castle-mound has been constructed by tiny, blind insects from particles of soil mixed with spit and shaped into tiny pellets. These tiny pellets are the only building material the termites have!

How does a tiny, blind worker termite know just where to add its pellet to create the complicated castle in which millions will live? No one knows. But behavior like this is very hard for people who believe in the Theory of Evolution to explain. Not only is there no way to explain the construction skills, but there is also no way to explain how termites could have survived before they developed the construction instinct! How much more reasonable to see in the termite community another example of the creativity and wisdom of our God.

Life inside the castle

Much has been learned about the way castle termites live together. Some termites venture outside to find food. The ones who venture out are workers. When they stumble onto a food source, these workers leave a scent trail for others to follow. This is necessary because the worker termites are blind.

There are different kinds of termites in the castle. Soldier termites guard any entrances and rush to defend the castle if a wall is broken into. The soldiers have such huge jaws that they cannot feed themselves, but must be fed by workers.

In the center of the castle lies the queen, who lays up to 30,000 eggs a day! These eggs and the larvae which hatch from them are also tended by workers.

Each of the different forms of termites produces pheromones. These are chemicals which have an odor. These pheromones, or smells, carry messages which circulate throughout the castle. One of the special messages has to do with which form of termites will be produced. You see,

the termite colony is special in that all its members are born from the eggs of the termite queen! The millions of insects are all offspring of a single queen termite.

Each form of termite has a special smell. If many soldier termites should be killed defending the castle, there will be less of the soldier smell (soldier pheromone) in the castle. The queen will then produce eggs that will develop into soldiers!

The complicated social structure and the use of pheromones to carry the messages that control the life of a termite colony are other instances of wonders it is hard for the Theory of Evolution to explain. But they are not a problem for those who believe in creation.

Dancers with wings

Bees are also insects that live in a community. They too seem to work together by instincts which we are only beginning to understand.

In the beehive also there is a single queen who gives birth to all the

Bees communicate the location of flowers by dancing for other worker bees.

community's members. Here too pheromones circulating within the hive are an important means of communication.

But worker bees have another fascinating way to communicate with each other. Worker bees are those who go out of the hive in search of nectar, the sweet liquid produced in flowers. When a bee finds a new flower filled with nectar, it carries all the nectar it can back home. And then it dances to tell other workers where to go to get more nectar.

The dance of the bee has been carefully studied. When a bee returns, it lands on a flat platform in front of the entrance of the hive. It dances a circle then cuts across the circle, while buzzing excitedly. The track it makes as it cuts across the circle points directly to the target flower! The workers who have carefully watched this dance then launch into the air and fly in the direction indicated.

The first bee then goes inside the hive, to dance some more. If the bee goes just a short way inside the hive, the flower will be near. The farther inside the hive the bee goes before it dances again, the further away the flower is. Again the bee dances in a circle. But this time the circle is made on the wall of the hive, for there is no flat floor on which to dance. When the bee dances on the wall, it also cuts across its circle. But now the angle of its dance shows watchers where the new flower is *in relation to the sun.*

If the flower can be found by flying directly toward the sun, the bee will cross the circle going straight up or down. If the flower is to the right of the sun, the bee will cut across the circle at just the angle that others must fly to find it.

Other workers in the hive watch closely, and then when they leave the hive, they remember the dance and always fly away in just the right direction.

Who taught the bees to dance? Who taught them to understand just what each dance means? How could such complicated behavior have just happened?

Nobel prize winner Albert Szent-Gyorgyi (1977) wrote of a much simpler relationship. He studied how a young herring gull could peck at a red spot on its parent's beak to get the adult to spit up food. While the action seems simple, this Nobel prize winner says "it involves a whole series of most complicated chain reactions with a horribly complex underlying nervous mechanism." Asked what the odds are that this behavior pattern could develop by chance, Szent-Gyorgyi says it "has the probability of zero."[1] Yet every example we've seen in this chapter is far more complicated than that of a young gull pecking at a red spot when hungry!

On the march

The ant is another insect that lives in colonies. There are many different kinds of ants, and there are many amazing patterns in ant behavior. One of the strangest patterns is found among South America's "army" and Africa's "driver" ants.

These ants march in columns, attacking and eating any living thing in their path. In some parts of the world it is dangerous to tie up an animal because if a column of army ants comes by, it will bite the animal to death and eat it.

The army ants march in a long column, with soldier ants at the head. Worker ants follow, many carrying the larvae of the next generation. These larvae give off a pheromone message. As long as the message-scent is given off, the army keeps on marching.

But when it is time for the larvae to hatch into ants, the army halts. The soldiers and workers find a place between tree roots or stones and literally *create a living nest from their own bodies*.

This living nest of clinging ants has rooms where the birthing infants can be placed. It has passageways along which others can travel, and a chamber for the queen. The queen begins to swell, and within a week, she starts to lay eggs. In a few days there are some 25,000 eggs in the living nest. At the same time, the birthing ants in the other rooms emerge, to become the workers who

Will insects like the feared army ants ever take over the world? No, because of a special feature of God's design found always—and only—in the insect world.

will carry the just laid eggs!

The army, with its 25,000 new recruits, many carrying the eggs of its next generation, marches off again, ready to attack, kill and eat.

Even the largest of animals run from army ants. The individual ant may be small. But enlisted in an army, the marching ant is one of the most feared of jungle creatures.

Will insects take over the world?

Science fiction movies have been made about giant ants or other insects taking over the world. Fiction stories too have been written, suggesting that atomic explosions might cause mutations in the insect world. Is it likely that insects will grow to monster size and threaten human life?

No—and for an interesting reason. While there are millions of kinds of insects, all have one common trait that limits their size. Insects have no lungs. Instead, they have breathing tubes that run the length of their bodies. These tubes draw oxygen from the air. While some insects have ways to pull air into the tubes, the longer the tube the less effective they are in providing the oxygen all living animals need.

Simply put, the way insects breathe means that they cannot grow to giant size and live! Larger insects would never be able to absorb the amount of oxygen they would need to keep them alive.

As Christians, we clearly see the hand of God here. The Lord did not create Earth to be mastered by insects, but to be a home for humankind. In his wisdom he designed insects with a built-in limitation that guarantees they will never supplant human beings as masters of his world.

Just For Fun

1 Evolutionists claim to believe that living things change into other forms that are new and different. If you were an evolutionist, would you worry that insects might develop lungs?

2 Which of the animal wonders in this chapter do you think is hardest for people who believe in the Theory of Evolution to explain?

3 Look up whales in an encyclopedia. What else can you learn about them that might be called a "wonder"?

4 What can you find in the Bible about ants? Look up ants in a concordance, and then read about them.

5 Each of the animals and insects mentioned in this chapter seems special. What do you think makes human beings special? What makes us important to God?

13 WHEN IT TAKES TWO

One of the hardest wonders for people who believe the Theory of Evolution to explain is called mutualism, or symbiosis. Many times in the plant and animal world, we find two different living creatures which live in strange relationships with each other. In many cases one, or both, could not even exist without the other!

Probably you enjoy many kinds of food. But no one I know would like to sit down to a dinner of pine boards or the roots of an oak tree.

Wood is mostly hardened cellulose. Cellulose is the major substance in all plants. But the plants we eat have other components as well. Wood, which is nearly pure cellulose, is too hard for us to eat. What's more, human beings cannot digest cellulose in any form.

Some insects, however, seem to enjoy munching on wood. Termites actually live almost exclusively on wood. Yet the fact is that *termites cannot digest cellulose either*!

How can termites, who eat wood, live on a food they can't digest? Well, wood-eating termites have tiny organisms called flagellates in their intestines. These tiny animals can live only in the absence of free oxygen. If they are left in the open air, they quickly die. What these organisms

What do polyps, the tiny animals that create coral reefs, have in common with soft, blind, land-dwelling termites? And how is that shared feature evidence of God?

can do, however, is digest wood! So when the termite eats his meal, it's the tiny animals living inside his body that digest it for him.

What happens if the two are separated? In an experiment, termites were exposed to extra oxygen to kill their flagellates. Then the termites were fed their usual lunch of wood. The termites ate the wood—but could not digest it. When the same termites were reinfected with the flagellates, they were again able to digest cellulose.

This is one of the many examples in nature of a symbiotic, or mutual, relationship. The termite could not live without the flagellate because it would be unable to digest the wood it eats and would starve to death. The flagellate, out of the intestine of the termite, would be poisoned by oxygen and die. Together, each lives. Separated, each will die!

Mutualism and symbiotic relationships are very difficult for the Theory of Evolution to explain. Clearly the termite could not have existed before the flagellate developed. And the flagellate could not have developed in the open air, away from the dark safety of the termite's intestine. So how could either one ever have existed without the other?

Yet to claim that each evolved from some other kind of animal, and evolved just in time to save each other's life, is rather hard to accept. When existence itself requires that two creatures live in a specialized, complicated relationship, the Theory of Evolution seems less reasonable than ever.

What is especially fascinating as we look at the world God created is to discover that many different kinds of mutual and symbiotic relationships are found in nature. Each is a quiet witness to the fact that God, not chance, is the best explanation for the world in which you and I live.

Mutualism in the oceans

Coral reefs are found throughout the warmer oceans of the world. These reefs are created by tiny animals called coral polyps. But the polyps have no bodily systems for getting rid of wastes or for extracting oxygen from the water. Instead the bodies of these small animals are filled with great numbers of even tinier plants! These tiny plants, algae, absorb the polyps' waste and produce proteins. The algae also use carbon dioxide produced by the animal, and in return the algae give off the oxygen the polyps need to exist. Without the tiny algae literally living in their bodies, the polyps would die.

Coral polyps live close to the surface of the sea and must have sunlight for them and their algae guests to live. But out in the depths there is another, even stranger, relationship.

No light from the sun can reach deeper in the ocean than about 375 feet. At that depth the water temperature is close to freezing. Only recently have scientists discovered that over 2,000 species of fish and as many kinds of other living creatures swim in depths that light never reaches.

But over half of these fish have their own light! Yet the fish do not produce the light themselves. Instead they have special pouches, near the eye or on the tail or a fin. In each pouch is a colony of thousands of bacteria. These bacteria give off a chemical glow.

It might remind you of the way a typical flashlight works. The flashlight contains *batteries* that provide the power for the light, just as the bacteria provide the fish's light.

What is even more interesting is that the fish are equipped with shutters, as we are with eyelids. When the fish choose, they can close their shutters and turn off their lights! And when they choose, they can open the shutters, just as you or I might switch on a flashlight.

Fish that live deep in the ocean carry light-giving bacteria in pouches under their skin. And they can turn these "lights" on and off at will.

No one is sure of the purpose of the bacterial flashlights carried by deep sea fish. One suggestion is that the lights might help males and females find each other and mate. Another is that the lights may be a lure to attract smaller fish that serve as food.

But whatever the purpose, we again have an unusual symbiotic relationship. The bacteria could never survive outside the pouches maintained for them by the fish. And it is likely that in some way not yet understood the tiny living flashlights make a life or death difference to their fishy hosts.

Insects and plants

There are many mutual relationships between insects and plants. Some of them are very unusual indeed.

The yucca moth and yucca plant have one of these unusual relationships. The yucca moth flies to the flower of the yucca plant (also called the Spanish bayonet). The moth collects pollen in special mouth pouches. She then flies to another flower. First she goes to the outside base of the flower and pokes a tiny hole in it to lay her single egg. The moth then flies up to the open flower. She crawls in the flower, down to its base, and there stuffs the ball of pollen she gathered earlier.

Later the plant will produce a great number of seeds. When the moth egg hatches, the larvae will eat some of these seeds. The rest of the seeds will be scattered, and some will grow to become new yucca plants.

Here is another example of two living creatures which simply could not exist without each other. The plant can only be pollinated (fertilized) by this moth. And the moth egg can only be deposited in the plant. Neither one could exist without the other.

Insects and orchids

Orchids are among the most exotic of flowers. They come in many different colors and shapes. But there is no life-or-death reason for insects to visit orchids, as there is for the yucca moth to visit the yucca.

Instead, orchids have many different ways to draw just the right insect to them. One orchid, that grows on Grand Bahama Island, has flowers that look just like a particular male insect. The real male insect sees this counterfeit in his territory! Angrily he attacks the flower and in the process is covered with pollen. When the insect sees another counterfeit male on another orchid, he attacks again, thus spreading the pollen from flower to flower!

Orchids are more than beautiful flowers. Their survival depends on their ability to trick insects into helping them reproduce.

Another orchid, called the Ophrys, is pollinated only by tiny wasps. The flower has a pheromone, a chemical smell, that is just like the pheromone of a female wasp. The counterfeit smell is so attractive that sometimes male wasps will fly right by female wasps to visit the orchid!

Another orchid has flowers that look just like female wasps, even to their shiny eye spots, wings, antennae and hairs! Again odor attracts the male wasp, who tries to mate with the flower. In the process the wasp is covered with pollen, which he will then take to another blossom.

Botanists, who study plants, have identified at least 65 different chemical compounds that orchids blend to attract insects. In most cases each kind of orchid will have its own smell, intended to attract just one kind of insect!

Orchids are often designed to make sure that once an insect is attracted it will pick up or leave pollen. Several orchids trap the bees they attract. The bees panic, but the flower encloses them in a roomlike structure for up to an hour and a half. When the bees calm down, they discover a narrow tunnel that is the only way out of the trap. As a bee crawls up the tunnel it must rub against the sides—and is covered with the orchid's pollen.

In the case of the special relationship between orchids and insects, there is no special benefit to the insect. The orchid is the one who needs the insect. How amazing that different kinds of orchids have just the right odors and just the right shapes to attract one insect who will pick up their pollen and carry it to other orchids of the same kind.

More mimics

When a flower or animal structure looks like something else, the similarity is called mimicry. For instance, some orchids grow flowers that mimic, or look like, male or female insects.

Sometimes mimicry helps save an animal's or insect's life. Geometrid moth wings have a pattern and color that make them look just like twigs. When they land on a branch, they hold their abdomen up in the air—at exactly the same angle as the other twigs that sprout from that branch. Sitting there they are almost impossible to distinguish from the branch.

Another moth, in South America, has a large round mark on each side of its head. When frightened, it waves its head from side to side—and looks just like a wide-eyed snake.

In our own country the monarch butterfly is safe from birds and other enemies. Quite simply, the monarch tastes bad to them. On the other hand, the viceroy butterfly has an attractive taste. But the viceroy butterfly looks so much like the monarch that most birds are fooled and leave the viceroy alone!

Not all mimics are attractive. One African plant mimics rotten meat in order to attract flies. The plant's flowers are wrinkled and brown and covered with hairs that look like decaying animal skin. The smell too is of rotting meat. The plant even warms its flower to the temperature of rotting meat. The flies are fooled so completely that they not only come to the flower but even lay their eggs on it, as they would have on actual rotting meat.

There are many examples of mimicry in the plant and animal world. In fact, there are so many, and these are so helpful to the mimics, that one text written by an evolutionist says, "It is tempting to think that mimics deliberately copy the models." He then goes on to say that, of course, we cannot suppose intelligence had anything to do with it. It must have been "a matter of chance."[1]

That writer is correct, of course, that the insects and plants involved

The pattern on the wings of the viceroy butterfly mimics the pattern of the monarch butterfly. For the viceroy, the imitation is a matter of life or death.

did not deliberately copy their models themselves. But the notion that the complicated patterns seen in mimicry just happened is even harder to imagine.

How sad that the writer, who realizes that mimicry seems to call for intelligent planning, fails to recognize mimicry as evidence of God. Mutualism and symbiosis in nature *do* show intelligent planning. They give evidence of design, and design is evidence of the existence of our God.

Wonders everywhere

The Theory of Evolution says that all living things developed from single, living cells. This happened by chance, by processes that no one can really explain.

Evolutionists have suggested different possible processes. Darwin believed traits that helped an organism survive were carried on and others were lost. But no evolutionist can tell where the original traits came from in the first place!

Modern Neo-Darwinists think that point mutations explain the process. They think small changes in genes took place by chance. Over millions of years these tiny changes added up, and this explains the many different living creatures in our world today. But this notion cannot explain the complex design and behaviors we see in the animal world. And it does not explain where the original genes and chromosomes came from.

Other scientists think that Evolution happened in jumps, as totally new creatures just happened to come from old ones. These "hopeful monsters" explain why no fossils that show gradual changes between different kinds of animals can be found in Earth's rocks. But no one can suggest how such a monster might happen—and no one has been able to cause this kind of change despite years and years of laboratory experiments.

Even though evolutionists can't explain how change from single cells to complex animals might have happened, they argue that it did. They point to changes in existing kinds of animals, such as the development of different breeds of dogs, as evidence. And they point to homology—similarities between living things—and say this too is evidence for the Theory of Evolution.

But as we've seen, evolution (with a small "e") does not prove Evolution (with a capital "E"). And there are much better explanations for similarities than are offered in any Theory of Evolution.

In fact, the Bible says that God in the beginning created the different "kinds" of plant and animal life. And each reproduces "more of its own kind." The things we find in nature, and the way that plants and animals keep on being the same kind of plants or animals despite small changes, shows how trustworthy the Bible is.

Many people do view the Theory of Evolution as a fact, rather than as an unproven theory. School textbooks present the Theory of Evolution as if it were proven. School teachers may even tell students that the Theory of Evolution is a fact and ridicule those who believe in creation. Yet the more we examine the wonders of nature, the more confident we are that the marvels of design we see there simply could not have just happened.

The woodpecker is designed specifically for his way of life and is different from all other birds. His feet and tail feathers enable him to stand upright on a tree's trunk; his beak has a shock absorber; his tongue is so long it curls around his skull. Design like this did not just happen. Everything bears the clear mark of planning.

The termite lives in a community of millions. Many live in giant castle mounds that these blind insects build from tiny grains of clay. The instincts that enable them to unerringly build air-conditioned, temperature-controlled structures simply cannot be explained by the Theory of Evolution.

The relationship between the termite and the tiny flagellate in its intestine is necessary if either is to survive. This amazing relationship, and the many mutual relationships between different living things, can hardly be explained as a result of chance mutations.

No, the wonders in our world are far better explained by creation. It is God who made the first "kinds" of plants and animal life. It is he who built into the original genes and chromosomes the ability to adapt and change, and yet to remain forever the same basic kind.

Wherever we look in nature we see evidence of design and planning. And, in design and planning, we see clear evidence of the existence of our God.

Just For Fun

1 Find a book on nature in your school or public library. Make a list of all the things you find that seem to call for intelligent design.

2 Look through the nature book again. Make another list of plants and/or animals which seem to need each other to live or reproduce.

3 Which of the things described in this chapter do you think is hardest for people who believe the Theory of Evolution to explain? Why?

4 Do some research on animal home-building. Look up one of these three: spider webs, beaver lodges, bird nests. What do you learn that might be evidence of God's hand in nature?

5 Read Psalm 104. How do you think we are to respond to the wonders that we find in the plants and animals that God has made?

HUMANITY IN GOD'S UNIVERSE

Then God said, "Let us make man in our image, in our likeness . . ."

14 THE FAMILY TREE?

Evolution and scripture are in direct conflict over one vital question: Who are human beings? Evolutionists say that people, like apes, evolved from some earlier animal form. The Bible says that God created human beings in his own image.

Maybe you've seen them: pictures of cavemen with squat, bent bodies and dull, beastlike features. Drawings of these "Neanderthal men" have appeared in magazines as well as in high school and college textbooks. Probably many adults even today think scientists have "proven" that creatures like these are the ancestors of modern human beings.

Where did this idea come from, and what is wrong with it? A number of fossil bones have been found in different parts of Europe. Scientists think some of them are as much as 100,000 years old. When the first few bones were found in 1856, evolutionists were anxious to prove their theory of human development. Working from just a few fragments, the scientists *misinterpreted* what they found and drew caveman pictures, showing what the supposed ancestors of modern humans looked like. And they said that their finds "proved" the "fact" of human evolution.

But who says that they misinterpreted the bones they found and that the caveman pictures they drew are wrong? No, it's not some scien-

tist who is a Christian and is eager to show that the evolutionary view is wrong. Here is what the *Encyclopedia Britannica* (15th edition) says in

For many years cavemen were pictured as bent, ugly creatures with animallike faces. But something has happened that changed the once-accepted idea of what Neanderthal men looked like!

its article on Neanderthal man:

> The popular conception that those people were slouched in posture and walked with a shuffling, bent-kneed gait seems to have been due in large part to faulty reconstruction of the skull base and to misinterpretation of certain features of the limb bones of one of the Neanderthal skeletons discovered early in the 20th century.

Today all paleontologists agree that the Neanderthals were true human beings who lived in Europe, not a "missing link" at all. They did not look like cavemen; they looked much more like the people who live in your own hometown! And the skulls show that they had as much or more brain capacity than we do.

But even though scientists know better, many people today still think that cavemen, whose pictures they saw in school, really existed. And they think the Neanderthal people were an animallike link in the chain of human evolution.

Piltdown man

In 1912 a skull found in Piltdown, England excited evolutionists. The skull was humanlike, but the jaw was like an ape. And near the skull were other fossils and even tools! Surely this was proof of human evolution!

For forty years the scientific community used the Piltdown man to demonstrate the "fact" of human evolution. Then, in the 1950s Piltdown was shown to be a hoax! Someone had taken a human skull and an ape jaw, stained them to make them look old, and had actually used a file to

HUMAN PREHISTORY ACCORDING TO JOHANSON

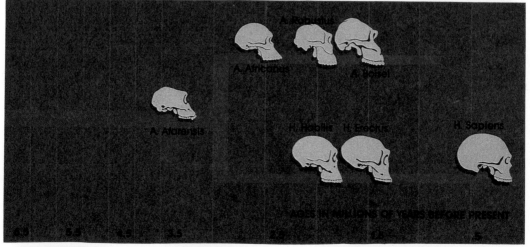

Paleontologists have said that apelike skulls found in Africa provide evidence about human Evolution. Two different theories had been presented—until the discovery of a new skull in 1985 showed *both* are probably wrong!

HUMAN PREHISTORY ACCORDING TO LEAKEY

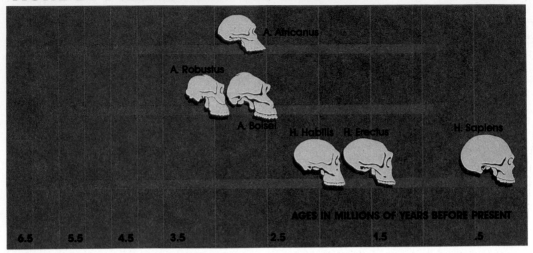

A. Africanus

A. Robustus

A. Boisei   H. Habilis   H. Erectus   H. Sapiens

AGES IN MILLIONS OF YEARS BEFORE PRESENT

| 6.5 | 5.5 | 4.5 | 3.5 | 2.5 | 1.5 | .5 |

make them fit! When reexamined, the tools too were obvious frauds! Many now suspect that the joke was played on evolutionists by the author of the Sherlock Holmes tales, Arthur Conan Doyle. We do know that the evolutionists were all too easily fooled.

Java man also fooled the scientific community. This "man" was constructed from a part of a skull and a leg bone found, a distance apart, in a gravel deposit on the Island of Java. Later the man who found the remains decided that the skull was human, but the leg bone was from a large gibbon ape!

Why did the discoverer, Eugene DuBois, change his mind about Java man? Because he also found a whole human skull in the same strata. The Java man could hardly be the ancestor of a human who lived at the same time. But DuBois kept that discovery secret for nearly thirty years, and many today still think the Java man "proves" the theory of human evolution!

Now, these and other mistakes in the interpretation of fossils do not *prove* that modern discoveries are misinterpretations, too. But they do remind us of an important point. When someone finds a few bones or bone fragments and announces to the world that he has found the link between human and animal, we don't *have* to believe him!

Even if nearly all scientists quickly agree, we needn't think that the theory of human evolution is a "fact." Even when newspapers and magazines echo the finder's claims, we'll be wise not to accept them.

Why? Partly because *every other claim to have discovered some link to man's animal past has later been proven wrong*! Yet each of these claims was widely accepted by scientists as a "fact" and was reported in newspapers and magazines as if it were true!

What's new?

The newest idea about humans is that both they and apes evolved in Africa from some early common ancestor. A number of skulls and bone fragments have been found in Africa. These *australopithecine* skulls are supposed to be of animals who evolved from that common ancestor of human beings.

Two scientists (Johanson and White), who have studied the skulls, think that one skull, given the name *afarensis*, was a common ancestor to human beings and to the other australopithecines (which have been named *africanus*, *robustus*, and *boisei*). Another group of scientists, headed by Richard Leakey, thinks that the common ancestor has not yet been discovered.

In 1985, however, a new skull called KNM-WT 17000 was discovered. Writing in *Discover* magazine (September, 1986), Pat Shipman, a paleontologist at the Johns Hopkins School of Medicine, said:

> What the new skull does, in a single stroke, is overturn all previous notions of early hominid evolution ... The things we thought we understood reasonably well we don't.

When Dr. Shipman explains further what this skull discovery might mean, she gives one reasonable explanation—which she does not want to accept.

We could assert that we have no evidence whatsoever of where *Homa* [human being] arises from and remove all members of the genus *Australopithecus* from the hominid family. . . . I've such a visceral, negative reaction to this idea that I suspect I am unable to evaluate it rationally. I was brought up on the notion that Australopithecus is a hominid.

What does she mean? Simply that paleontologists have discovered evidence *against* even the newest theory of human evolution! Once again what scientists and newspapers have been presenting as "facts" have turned out to be little more than another misinterpretation!

Yet even the discoverers of the new fossil do not *want* to accept what it means! They have been "brought up" to believe the myth of human evolution and to accept the theories of mere men.

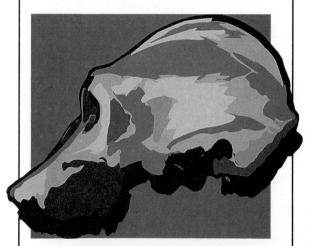

This is an illustration of a skull called KNM-WT 17000. It was discovered in 1985 and has made scientists admit "the things we thought we understood reasonably well we don't."

Why so many mistakes?

Why is the history of attempts to trace the supposed evolution of human beings so filled with misinterpretations and mistakes? One obvious reason is that many skulls are reconstructions of how the discoverer *thinks* the bone pieces might fit together. The picture of *afarensis*, the key fossil in the theory of both Johanson and White and of Richard Leakey, helps us understand. Only the light brown-colored bones and teeth were actually found. The blue part is imagination! It is how the finders *think* the rest of the skull *might* have looked!

When so much of a key fossil is a product of imagination—and the skull and face may not even come from the same skeleton—it's not surprising when theories based on it are later shown to be wrong!

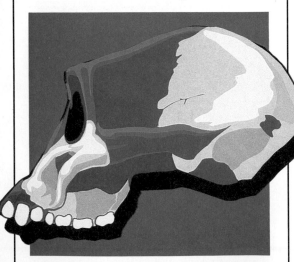

This drawing shows the key skull reconstruction of *afarensis*. But do the braincase and jaw really fit together this way or not?

Yet the key reason for misinterpretation of fossils is the idea that apes and people evolved in the first place! Belief in Evolution is what has led paleontologists to call the bones they find *hominid* (a word which means in the line of man).

What is most fascinating, however, is that the same scientists who search for fossil ancestors of modern man give the fossil bones they find a name like *Australopithecus*. Why is this fascinating? Because *pithecus* means "ape" or "apelike"! The striking thing about these fossils is that they are *so* apelike. In fact 95% of this key fossil is monkeylike!

Why then aren't the bones simply recognized as fossil bones of extinct apes? Ultimately because the finders believe in Evolution and *want* the bones they find to reveal a link between modern humans and the ancestors of apes.

Right now, the accepted theory of how human evolution took place is being shaken by the discovery of KNM-WT 17000. What can we expect in the future? We can expect that during your lifetime you'll read of many fossil discoveries of "early man." Scientists and newspapers will report these discoveries as further proof of Evolution—just as they reported the Neanderthal man, the Piltdown man, the Java man and now Australopithecus.

In time, other newer discoveries will probably show that the scientists and the newspapers were wrong, and another even newer theory will emerge, to prove again that human beings evolved.

When each new Theory of Evolution is presented, you will know better! You'll remember *that not one fossil brought forward as a "missing link" has ever been one*, but each in its turn has been proven to be something else!

Where did humans really come from?

The answer is found in the Bible. There came a time, after God had created the world and made it beautiful, that he was ready for his most important creation of all! Genesis tells us,

> Then God said, "let us make man in our image, in our likeness, and let them rule over the fish in the sea and the birds of the air, over the livestock, over all the earth, and over all the creatures that move along the ground."
>
> Genesis 1:26

> And so the Lord God formed the man from the ground and breathed into his nostrils the breath of life, and the man became a living being.
>
> Genesis 2:7

There are many things in this account that help us understand who we human beings really are.

First, we understand that God himself made us in a separate and special act of creation. People did not evolve from some lower kind of animal at all.

Second, we understand that God made us different from every other living thing. Our bodies are physical, made of elements found on Earth. In this, we are similar to animals. But there are many important differences, too. God simply spoke, and the plants and animals were created. For human beings, God personally shaped our physical nature from the elements in the ground.

Third, the Bible says that God chose to make human beings in his own "image and likeness." This means that human beings have a spiritual part as well as a physical part. This is an important difference between human beings and animals.

Evolutionists look at the bones of human beings and apes, or the bones of modern men and fossil bones, and argue that because the bones are like each other in some ways, humans and animals are really the same. The evolutionist says that similarities prove humans and apes are both just animals, and the only difference is that humans have larger brains.

Yet this argument from physical similarity is foolish. It is not just that similarities of skeleton do not prove relationship (something we learned in chapter 10). What is most foolish is to think that it is our bones that make us human!

Trying to prove relationship by looking at fossil bones makes sense to evolutionists who believe that the human body evolved from earlier animals. But it does not answer the really important question: where did the heart, soul—the *nature*—of humans come from?

What I mean is this. Human beings are obviously different inside from all

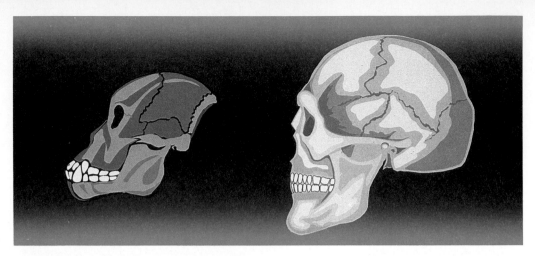

Is the real difference between the human and the ape found in the skeleton—or is the main difference not found in the *physical* nature at all?

other animals, no matter how similar bones or bodies might be. We human beings can appreciate beauty and paint a beautiful picture. We can imagine new things and then build them. We don't live by instinct. Instead, we learn and remember and pass on what we learn to the next generation. People can also communicate, thinking and talking about complex things.

Human beings also have a moral nature. We have a capacity for love and self-sacrifice. We are aware of right and wrong and can make good choices. And all human societies also are aware of the spiritual. People know that there is something beyond what we can see that is to be worshiped.

All this is so unlike what we find in animals that the *differences* between human and animal are amazingly clear.

The evolutionist thinks that the body of humans evolved from animals. But where does he think the

mind and heart and soul of humans came from?

In psychology books it is not unusual for evolutionists to speak of crime and wars and the evils people do as things that come from supposed "brute ancestors." Many evolutionists have tried to explain the bad in human beings in this way. Someday, they think, we will evolve further and be rid of our "animal instincts."

But evolutionists who write this way haven't stopped to ask *if the "bad" in humans came from our animal ancestors, where did the "good" come from?* Usually they don't ask about where the good things human beings can do came from. They don't wonder about all the abilities we have that no animal on Earth possesses. Yet it is obvious that all our human traits and abilities must have come from *somewhere*. They really could not have just happened!

For Christians, the Bible provides

the obvious answer. All the good and wonderful things that make human beings different came from God! God created us special. The things that make human beings special are ours only because God made us in his image, to be like him.

Either, or

While some Christian scientists think that God might have used evolution to fill our Earth with living creatures, they do *not* think that humans evolved. The conflict between the Bible and the theory of human evolution is just too clear.

Evolution says that humans are just animals that can think, who developed by chance out of earlier but different animals. The Bible teaches that human beings were made separately from the animals, by a special act of God.

Evolutionists look at the bones of humans and of some animals and say the similarities prove their theory. But anyone can look at the many, many ways in which people are different from animals, and realize that we and animals are *not* the same.

All the special things that set humans apart from the animal world confirm what the Bible says. God himself made us. And he made us to be like him.

Just For Fun

1 Look over chapter 10 again. What are the reasons why similarity (homology) does not prove relationship?

2 Read in an encyclopedia about Neanderthal man, Piltdown man or Java man. What do you learn that seems important? Why do you think people believed for so long that these remains "proved" the Theory of Evolution?

3 Look at the skull pictures in this chapter. Do any of them look human to you? How are they similar to human skulls? How are they different?

4 Make a list of ways that people are different from animals. Then check over your list. How many of these ways are physical (such as people have larger brains)? How many of these ways are "spiritual" (such as people can appreciate beauty)?

5 If someone told you that scientists have found human fossils that prove Evolution, what might you say to him or her? How would you argue that the facts better fit the Bible's account of man's special creation by God?

15 AMAZING AND WONDERFUL

Today doctors have learned many things about our human bodies. The more we learn about them, the more we realize that King David was right when he praised God because "you made me in an amazing and wonderful way. What you have done is wonderful" (Psalm 139:14, ICB).

David, thinking about how he was born and the body he was given, wrote a psalm of praise to God. Here is what he says in Psalm 139:13-16 (ICB),

You [God] made my whole being.
  You formed me in my mother's
    body.
I praise you because you made me
  in an amazing and wonderful way.

What you have done
  is wonderful.

I know this very well.

You saw my bones be-
  ing formed as I took
  shape in my mother's
  body.

When I was put together
  there, you saw my
  body as it was
  formed.

All the days planned for
  me were written in
  your book before I was
  one day old.

Like each of us, this baby grew from a single cell and will grow up to have an amazing and wonderful body.

Life in this world

God himself created Adam. Genesis tells us he shaped Adam's body from the dust of the earth. And then God breathed a special life into that body (Genesis 2:7).

The human body was designed for living on our Earth. But the special life that God gave only to human beings makes it possible for each of us to be a person who is very different from Earth's animals. In this chapter we'll look at the body God formed for us and realize, as David did long ago, that it didn't just happen.

We have been created by God. And the body God gave us is amazing and wonderful.

You and your body

Your body is a true marvel. You're aware of parts of your body: you can close your eyes and tell where your arms or legs are.

You have senses that tell you about the world around you. Your eyes send you messages about the world; your nose and ears send you messages, too. Sense receptors on your skin warn you if you get too close to something hot or if you bump into a hard object.

Most of these senses are designed to keep you in touch with the things outside your body. But inside your body there are many things happening of which you have no awareness at all. Food moves through your body automatically. Your blood cells fight diseases without any conscious directions from you. Your heart beats regularly without your even thinking about it.

When we look at all the systems built into our bodies, we realize again that it couldn't just happen. Our bodies and their systems have been carefully designed by God.

Inside your body

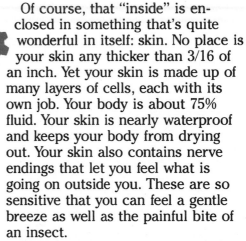

You generally know what is going on outside your body. You generally are not aware of what is going on inside.

Of course, that "inside" is enclosed in something that's quite wonderful in itself: skin. No place is your skin any thicker than 3/16 of an inch. Yet your skin is made up of many layers of cells, each with its own job. Your body is about 75% fluid. Your skin is nearly waterproof and keeps your body from drying out. Your skin also contains nerve endings that let you feel what is going on outside you. These are so sensitive that you can feel a gentle breeze as well as the painful bite of an insect.

The ability of your skin to sense what is going on outside is very important. The terrible disease of leprosy destroys the ability of the skin's nerves to feel. As a result the leper's fingers and toes are literally worn away, just as if they had been sandpapered down. Unable to feel what he or she touches, the leper does not know when something harms his hands or feet.

The skin also helps regulate your temperature. When you are too hot, tiny blood vessels in the skin open up and heat radiates away from your body. When you are cold, these blood vessels shut down and your body keeps heat in. And, the skin is your first line of defense against injury and disease germs.

The skin then is an amazing envelope that protects the equally amazing systems that exist within.

The world's best pump

One of the organs that you do not consciously control is your heart. That heart will pump about seventy-two times a minute, or 40,000,000 times a year! It pumps on whether you're awake or asleep. If you exercise, it will pump faster. If you're resting, it will slow down. It makes all these adjustments automatically, without your even being aware of them.

At its full size, your heart will be about the size of a fist and weigh from 1/2 to 3/4 of a pound. Yet each day it does enough work to lift your body a mile straight up! Every day an adult heart pumps blood through 75,000 miles of blood vessels! In fact, it pumps enough to fill a 4,000 gallon tank car every day. In a normal lifetime, your heart will pump about 450,000 *tons* of blood.

The heart is the most powerful muscle in your body. It is twice as strong as an athlete's leg muscles or

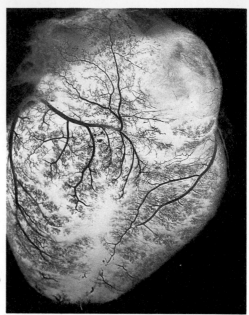

Your heart is the best, most trustworthy pump in the world. In just one year it pumps 40,000,000 times.

the arms of a weight lifter. But if the leg or arm muscles had to work constantly, as the heart muscle does, they would be exhausted in minutes!

There are several things we can do to keep our hearts strong. Eating non-fatty foods is important. So is exercise. And it is important not to smoke cigarettes because it harms the nerves that tell the heart muscle when to contract. And that can cause serious heart problems. So while we don't need to think about making our hearts beat, we do need to make good choices about how we treat our bodies.

The oxygen exchange

The lungs are also important inner organs. Each lung hangs in its own sealed compartment in your chest, and the lung of an adult weighs only about one pound.

The lung has no muscle at all. When we breathe, our chest muscles expand and the lungs expand in the vacuum this creates. Air is drawn into the lungs through the nose and a four-inch windpipe. The air rushes through millions of tiny air passages 1/100 of an inch in diameter and into even tinier air sacs.

Each of these air sacs is covered with tiny capillaries—blood vessels

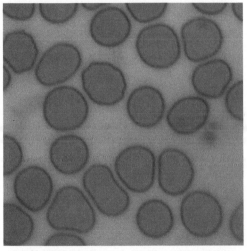

Red cells are carried in the blood throughout the body. They pick up oxygen in the lungs and carry it to every cell in the body.

so small that red blood cells must pass through one at a time.

As each red cell passes through its capillary, its load of carbon dioxide is released into the air sac, and it picks up a load of oxygen from the fresh air in the lung. When the blood cell starts into the capillary, it is blue; when it comes out, it is bright red.

It is very important that the lungs be kept clean and healthy, and the

air that reaches them should be warm and moist. As soon as you take a breath, an air cleaning process begins. Hairs in your nose trap large dust particles. The moist passage traps more. But the key cleaners are *cilia*, tiny hairs you can see only through a microscope. There are tens of millions of them in your air passages, and they wave twelve times a second, pushing captured dust and dirt up away from your lungs.

This is important because if dust or dirt fills up the lungs, they can hold less air, and less of the oxygen exchange you need to live can take place.

Like your heart, your lungs work automatically. Blood cells are carried automatically to capillaries that pass through air sacs, and the millions of *cilia* keep on working minute after minute, and day after day. There is very little you can do consciously to affect the way your body is at work.

But, again, there are choices you can make that affect your lungs and their health. Exercise makes you breathe in more deeply; without deep breathing the lungs lose some of their capacity for oxygen exchange.

Cigarette smoking is a great enemy of your lungs. Most people know that cigarettes cause lung cancer. But most don't know that cigarette smoke paralyzes the *cilia* that clean the air going to the lungs. Even worse, if a person smokes regularly for even two weeks, those tiny hairs *will begin to disappear!* Dust and dirt as well as smoke will get into your lungs. Healthy lungs are a bright pink color. The lungs of people who smoke soon become dark and grey. Smoking is the main reason why so many people today have terrible lung diseases and often die from them.

But there is another thing about our bodies. If a person stops smoking, those tiny little hairs *begin to come back*! We are amazingly and wonderfully made.

Rushing rivers within

If you cut yourself, you're sure to be aware of that special fluid that flows inside—your blood. But unless you're sick or injured, your bloodstream is something else you are not consciously aware of. It keeps on doing its work without any thought on your part.

It's hard to imagine how complex your bloodstream is. First, an adult has about 75,000 *miles* of blood vessels in his or her body! These vessels are pipes—arteries, veins and capillaries—that carry blood to *every cell* in the body.

It's as if a paperboy had a route 75,000 miles long and had some sixty trillion customers. That route would take you around the Earth three times—and you would have 16,000 times as many customers as there are people on our planet!

This river of blood flows constantly, taking fresh oxygen and food to the body's cells and removing carbon dioxide and other waste products. It is the red cells in the blood that do this particular work. Although red blood cells last only about 120 days, each will pass through the heart and visit other

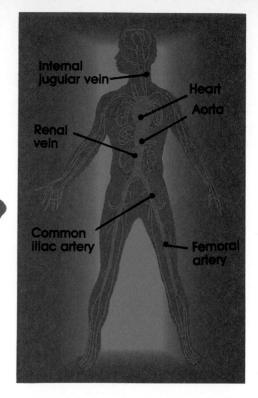

There are 75,000 miles of blood vessels that carry blood to the 60 trillion cells of the adult body. Arteries carry blood from the heart. Veins carry blood to the heart.

parts of the body 75,000 times!

Red cells are not the only cells in the bloodstream. There are many different kinds of white blood cells. They carry many different substances in the blood. Among them are sugars, salts, minerals, hormones, enzymes, amino acids, fats and others. All these float in a clear liquid called plasma and are carried along as the heart pumps blood through the body.

There are so many things that are amazing about this inner river of blood that is the body's transportation system. For one thing, cells need many different substances to remain healthy. Each cell will set up a coded "dock" when it has a need. And just the substance it needs will be attracted to that "dock" and stop there as it passes by in the bloodstream.

For another thing, certain kinds of white blood cells fight any disease germs or viruses that might be in the body. These cells, called *antibodies*, are specially designed to fight just one kind of invader—one kind of germ or infection. When a particular enemy germ gets inside the body, your blood system acts like a chemical laboratory. It quickly develops an antibody to fight that particular disease and immediately goes to work turning out hundreds of thousands of them.

There are close to a million different antibodies in an adult. Each one is specially designed to attack just one kind of enemy invader! And once your body has fought a particular disease, the antibodies in your blood remember it, even years later. If any germs or viruses of that disease get into the body, the right antibodies will attack it immediately. That's why if you have a disease like mumps or chicken pox as a child, you will not get it as an adult. The antibodies will "remember" the disease and attack its germs before they can make you sick.

How many cells in your body?

1= 260,000,000,000.

There are other inner systems besides the skin and heart and lungs and bloodstream that are amazing, too. Your digestive system trans-

forms the food you eat into the chemicals that nourish the body. Your liver cleanses your body. Glands send chemical signals through your body, and there are reproductive organs. All these truly are wonders.

But perhaps one of the most striking things about your body is where all the complex systems came from.

Just think for a minute. Each human being begins as a single cell, formed by the joining of a father's sperm and a mother's egg. From the one tiny cell comes a body that will have at least 26,000,000,000 cells.

What is more, that one original cell contained the code to make the thousands of *different kinds* of cells found in our bodies. Some of our billions of cells will be fat cells. There will be bone cells, heart muscle

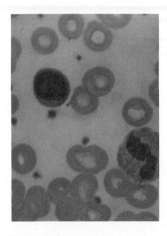

The blood also carries white cells that fight disease in your body. Your body may have a million kinds of white antibodies, each designed to fight just one kind of germ or virus.

cells, brain cells and lung cells. There will be cells that make up veins and capillaries, red blood cells and many different kinds of white blood cells. There will be different kinds of skin cells and tiny *cilia* cells growing on the cells that make up your breathing tubes. In your eyes there will be cells so transparent that you can see through them as if they were glass.

All this will come from one tiny original cell, which contained the code needed to make you a complete human being.

Eyes to see

There are other bodily systems that we are more aware of than our heart and lungs and bloodstream. One that we treasure is our eyes. How important to be able to see what is happening in the world around us!

This system too is amazing in its design. The eye is no larger than a ping pong ball, but it has so many millions of tiny electrical connections that it can handle 1 1/2 *million* messages at the same moment!

The eye's clear cornea organizes light rays. The oval, crystalline lens

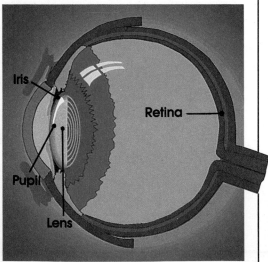

Iris

Retina

Pupil

Lens

The eye has 137 million special cells that respond to light and send messages to the brain, which enables us to see.

becomes fatter or flatter for near and far vision. Two other chambers of the eye are filled with fluid. These are clear fluids, so light can pass through them.

The light that comes into the eye is focused by the lens so that it falls on the retina. This is a thin, paper-like wall that covers the back of the eye. Although it is less than an inch square the retina has 137 *million* special cells that are sensitive to light. About 130 million of them are rod shaped. These rods are for black and white vision. The remaining seven million are shaped like cones. These permit us to see color.

All these cells receive impressions from the light that enters the eye. Each is connected to the optic nerve and sends tiny electric signals to that nerve and along it into the brain. These signals travel about 300 miles an hour! There, in the brain, the signals are interpreted so that we "see" pictures of what is in front of us. This complex system too is a mix of many different kinds of cells, each with its own special characteristics and job to do.

Ever new

HARD HAT AREA

There is even more. We learned earlier that red blood cells live only about 120 days. Actually, most cells in your body are constantly being replaced—even while your body keeps on working. Many kinds of cells live for only a few months before they die and are replaced.

This too is amazing when we stop to think about it. Imagine workmen constantly repairing your house while you tried to live in it. A carpenter rips up one board and replaces it with another while you're trying to sleep. An electrician turns off the power while you're trying to cook supper because he has to replace a wire. A painter slops blue paint on your shirt while you try to read in the living room. No, you can't constantly repair a house while people are living in it.

But your body is constantly repairing itself—and you don't even notice. Thousands of red blood cells are replaced every minute, without the flow ever being shut down. The cells in your heart are replaced, but that living pump never misses a beat. Your lungs, your eyes and your stomach are constantly being renewed, and you aren't even aware of it.

All this is possible because your body is so wonderfully made that, without any conscious direction from you, everything will be taken care of automatically. Yes, through your senses you are aware of what is going on outside. Your sight and your hearing, your ability to taste and smell and feel, all are amazing. But even more amazing are the things you and I are *not* aware of—the things that happen all the time in the bodies that God designed when he created Adam and formed Eve, the parents of our human race.

Just For Fun

1 Look up any two inner parts of your body in an encyclopedia or medical book. What do you learn about them that seems amazing and wonderful?

2 Why do you suppose God gave us senses to make us aware of the things outside our body, but not of what happens within?

3 Read Psalm 94:9. What do the senses God gave us tell us about him?

4 Each pound of fat a person carries in his body adds about 200 *miles* of blood vessels to the blood system and makes the heart work that much harder. Keeping our weight under control is one way we can help the automatic systems of the body work as God intended. What other things can we do?

5 If you were to write a praise psalm to God about your body, as David did, what would you write? What things in this chapter seem most wonderful and amazing to you and help you realize that you were created by God?

16 IN GOD'S IMAGE

The inner world of our bodies is an amazing one. Thousands of hidden systems work within us to keep our trillions of cells – and us – healthy and well. But even more amazing is the fact that you are *you*: an individual with your own memories, beliefs and identity.

Three times the Bible speaks of people acting like "an animal" (Psalm 73:22; Titus 1:12; 2 Peter 2:12). What makes the difference between a human being and an animal? One of these verses says that such people, like animals, "act without thinking." In another version of the Bible it says that they are "creatures of instinct." Animals do not think about the choices they make. They act on instinct or are trained by human beings. Only we human beings can stop and think about the choices we have to make.

Stopping to think about a choice is a very complicated thing. Suppose that your mom tells you not to take one of the fresh cookies she's made. But they smell so good! Your mouth starts to water, and suddenly you feel terribly hungry. It would be so easy just to reach out and take one.

But then you stop to think. Mom said not to take any. Of course, she might not miss just one. But even if she didn't miss one, it wouldn't be right to take the cookie. Besides, maybe she counted them. Maybe they're for a party or something special. She'd be really upset if you spoiled all the work she'd done. Finally you decide not to take a cookie, even though you really want one because you know it's right to obey your mom.

When you make that decision to obey your mom, you do something special. Your first instinct is to take a cookie, to act on the message of your senses—the delicious look and

Your ability to decide not to taste forbidden cookies helps prove that human beings are more complex than just our bodies and physical desires.

smell and imagined taste. But you don't act on it. Instead you think about your choice, and finally you decide *against* that first instinct.

Our ability to think about choices is associated with our brain. This also is an amazing organ, far more complex than the brain of animals. But even its uniqueness cannot explain *you* as the special, individual person that you are.

How does the brain work?

The brain is another organ that seems small. It weighs only two to

Neurons in the brain have many tiny threads that lie near others. Yet neurons never touch each other! Their chemical/electrical signals jump like sparks across the gap between them.

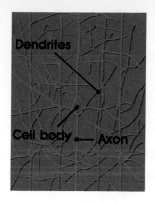

Dendrites

Cell body — Axon

three pounds. Yet it has some 30 billion cells called *neurons*, and five to ten times as many *glial* cells. So in your one brain, there are many times more cells than there are people in the world!

Several things make brain cells special. Brain cells, unlike other cells, are never replaced. They stay with you all your life. Perhaps the most interesting thing, however, is the way your brain cells are connected to each other. Each of your 30 billion neurons is connected with other neurons. Some of them connect as many as 60,000 times! This makes it possible for tiny electric messages to pass between brain cells quickly and in very complex ways. Your brain is far more complex than even the most complicated computer ever imagined.

Your nervous system

Cerebrum (right hemisphere)

Cerebrum (left hemisphere)

Cerebellum

Spinal cord

The brain is the most complex of our organs. Its three message centers control our bodies' systems, our voluntary actions, and our ability to remember, think and choose. But as a person created by God you are more than your brain.

Special nerve cells connect parts of your body to your brain. These cells are bundled up together in fibers, like telephone wires. They

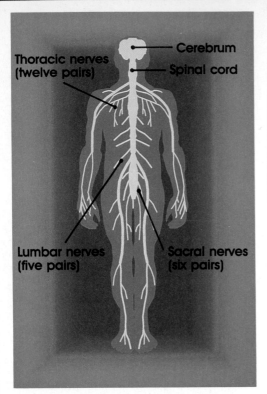

Thoracic nerves
(twelve pairs)

Cerebrum

Spinal cord

Lumbar nerves
(five pairs)

Sacral nerves
(six pairs)

The complex nervous system and other parts of our amazing human body explain how we can live in this world. But even the wonderful, physical systems God gave us can't explain how each individual is a person, with special abilities that are like God's.

carry messages from parts of your body to the brain, and they carry instructions from the brain back to the parts of your body. Many of these messages travel along the nervous system at 300 miles an hour!

The brain has three main message centers. The lowest part of the brain, called the *medulla oblongata* is responsible for automatic things like breathing and your heart beating. It receives messages from your inner organs and sends back instructions designed to keep your body well. Although you are not aware of them, millions of messages and instructions are handled by this part of your brain all the time.

The *cerebellum* is associated with voluntary actions. These are things you consciously choose to do, like walk or write or pick up a telephone.

The *cerebrum* is the largest and most important part of the human brain. It is here that messages from your eyes, ears and other senses are received and understood. This part of the brain is also associated with consciousness, memory, reasoning and those other special abilities that are distinctly human.

Each of these three message centers both receives and sends messages through the system of nerves that runs throughout your body.

Many scientists think that everything you or I experience through our entire life is stored as a memory in the brain, even things we can't recall. In fact, each memory seems to be stored in several different places, not just one.

The brain is the best protected organ in the body, placed inside the bony skull. This is very important as the brain itself is soft and jellylike. The fibers of the nervous system are also protected. They run down a channel built into the backbone.

Grey matter?

The brain is often spoken of as "grey matter." This is because the wrinkled outer layer of the brain is grey, while the inner core is white. The human brain is also folded and wrinkled on the outside. Without the folds, people would have about 30 times less brain surface. Even the highest animals have almost smooth brains, without folds and wrinkles.

There are many amazing things about our brains. For instance, the brain does not get tired, as muscles do. Also, we do not use all of the brain power that we have. Some think that people use only 10% to 15% of their brains for thinking. Our mental powers grow with use. The more you use your mind and the more you learn, the easier it is to think and learn. And, no matter how old you become, you can continue to learn and grow. It is true that sometimes sickness or injury makes it harder for older people to think and remember. But people can be bright and alert into their nineties and beyond.

Usually people measure ability to think and learn on an IQ (intelligence quotient) scale. But IQ does not automatically increase with brain size or even with the number of wrinkles on the brain. Besides, the most important thing isn't how smart a person is. What's most important is how you use the brain you have been given! A person who wants to learn and who studies is much better off than a person with a high IQ who does not study.

One Yale psychologist, Dr. Catharine Cox Miles, says that some of the most important people in history had only ordinary IQs. She lists some very famous people: Abraham Lincoln, the writer Ralph Waldo Emerson, the French general Napoleon. What these people had was the personal determination to work hard and keep on trying. Their character was far more important than their IQ.

The brain is so complex and amazing that it is simply unbeliev-able to imagine its specialized cells and connections could have evolved. Yet it is even more amazing to realize that each person who has ever lived is a separate, different, unique individual, with his or her own character and identity.

The uniqueness of every human being, as well as the wonders of the human body, is a witness to our creation by God. It is evidence you are more than your body and more than those tiny electrical charges flowing through your most complex organ.

The true you

You have your own body, with its own heart and lungs, its own senses and its own brain. In one sense your body is you. Burn your finger, and *you* feel pain. Swim, and *you* sense the water swishing against you. But you are far more than what you feel or experience through that body of yours.

You are a special and unique person. There never was and never will be another person just like you. Others will have brains and hearts and lungs. But no one else could have your personality, your memories, your character.

Yet there are other things you share with other human beings besides a human body. The Bible tells us that when God created people he said, "Let us make man in our image, in our likeness" (Genesis 1:26). God made our bodies from the "dust of the ground" so that we might live on Earth, in the physical universe. But God also "breathed in his nostrils the breath of life, and the man became a living being" (Genesis 2:7).

Our bodies connect us with the Earth and material things. In many ways our bodies are similar to the bodies that God gave animals, that make them able to live in the physical world, too.

But God gave us *more* than our physical bodies. God made us persons, and as persons, we are like God himself in many special ways.

What are some of these ways? Genesis tells us that after God created Adam, he planted a special garden in Eden for Adam to live in. The Bible says that there "the Lord God made all kinds of trees grow out of the ground—trees that were pleasing to the eye . . ." (Genesis 2:9). God then is someone who sees and appreciates beauty. People too can look at what God has created, or at a painted picture, and think of it as beautiful.

Genesis tells us that after each day of creation God looked at what he had done and called it "good." God felt satisfied and pleased by what he had accomplished. When God placed Adam in the Garden of Eden, he gave him work to do. God told Adam he could care for the garden (Genesis 2:15). God knew that human beings also would find satisfaction in doing good work.

Genesis also tells us that God let Adam name the animals (Genesis 2:19). God had great joy in creating. By letting Adam name the animals, he let Adam find joy in discovering and doing something new just as he had.

Later, Adam realized that although

Because God made human beings like himself, we can appreciate beauty and do many other wonderful things. But perhaps most importantly, we can make moral choices between what is right and wrong.

Eden contained many wonderful gifts, something was lacking. Adam was lonely without a helper who was just right for him. Then God caused Adam to sleep, and God formed Eve, the first woman, from Adam's rib. Eve, though different from Adam in some ways, was a person just as Adam was. At last Adam had a person like himself to love and care for, a person with whom to share work and beauty and joy. God knew that Adam, and each of us, needs others to love and to share with.

What does it mean for us to be persons and for God to be a person? Partly it means to be an individual who is able to think, to remember, to appreciate beautiful things, to create new things. Partly it means to feel emotions like joy and love, caring and pity. It means to be like God in these ways, although we are not like God in other ways. These gifts of being a person do not come from our bodies or even our brains. They come as a special gift from God who made us in his own image.

What evolutionists can never explain

In an earlier chapter we saw that similarities between kinds of animals (homology) does not prove they came from a common animal ancestor. But evolutionists think that, because the human body is similar in some ways to the bodies of animals, people and modern animals both evolved. Some evolutionists even try to explain wars and crime as something left over from "our animal ancestors" because many animals kill what they eat.

But evolutionists have no answer when asked where the special things that make us so different from the animals came from. What about the ability to appreciate beauty? What about the ability to paint a picture or compose lovely music? What about the ability to invent things like airplanes, spaceships, TV and computers?

These are ours only because God gave human beings special gifts when he shared his image and likeness with us.

A person who refuses to believe in God has no explanation for the wonderful things that make human beings different from every other creature in the world.

God's gift?

If human beings were to be truly like God, there was one other capacity people must be given. God is a moral being. He knows right from wrong and chooses what is right. To be like God, people also must be able to make moral choices.

This is why God planted one special tree in the Garden of Eden and then commanded Adam not to eat its fruit. "If you ever eat fruit from that tree," God warned Adam, "you will surely die" (Genesis 2:17). Adam and Eve had a very clear choice to make. They could obey God and do what was right. Or they could disobey God and do what was wrong. As long as they did what was right, they would be close to the Lord, and their bodies would not die.

Sometimes we may think that the tree God planted in Eden was a trick or that God was trying to trap Adam. It wasn't like that at all. If Adam was to be a person like God, he *must* make moral choices.

We don't know how many times Adam and Eve passed by that tree and chose not to eat its fruit. They may have made right choices for many years. But one day Satan confused and fooled Eve, and she ate. Then Adam decided to disobey God. He too ate the forbidden fruit.

At that moment their bodies began to grow old and die, just as our bodies do today. And at that moment Adam and Eve "knew good and evil," just as we do, and the temptation to do things that are not right. Adam and Eve had sinned.

Every human being who has ever lived has also sinned and chosen to do things he or she knows are wrong. That is why Jesus, God's Son, was born into the world and died on the cross. He died to pay for our sins and to offer us forgiveness. He died too so that we might be truly good, so that in trusting him we might find strength to make right choices every day.

Do you remember at the beginning of this chapter the story about the young person's seeing and smelling some delicious cookies and then deciding to do what his mom had said and not take any? Well, this story illustrates the moral sense God gives human beings. That moral sense makes us very different from animals.

We often know what is right but want to do wrong. If we do what we know is wrong, we will feel guilty and ashamed. But we also can stop and think and decide to do what we know is right. Then, even though we deny ourselves a thing we wanted, we feel good about doing what is right.

We have guilty feelings when we do what is wrong, and we have good feelings when we do what is right. These feelings are special reminders that God made human beings in his image. We are not just animals, but we have been made special by God so that we can know and love him and choose right instead of wrong.

You, for always

Although you have a heart and lungs and brain and all those other body parts, you are more than your body. You are a special, distinct person. You are your thoughts, your beliefs, your memories, your friendships, your choices and your character as much as you are a body.

What's more, the Bible teaches us that the true you—that *person* who is different from every other person who ever lived—will exist forever! Your body may grow old and die. But you will not stop then. You will still be yourself. You will still be able to think and remember, still be conscious and aware. This too is part of being made in God's image. We are far more important to God than to simply stop existing when our bodies die.

This is one of the most important reasons why we can't believe in the Theory of Evolution. That theory teaches that people, like animals, are only their bodies. When the body dies, the person just stops existing.

The Bible teaches that people are so special to God that he created us differently from the other living things. God gave us bodies, but he also made us persons, with all the special abilities that persons have. And, God made us special to him. God loves us so much that he wants us to live with him, forever and ever.

Jesus died for our sins so that we might be able to live with God forever, as well as live good lives here on earth. Only when we believe what the Bible says about who we are will we have any reason to think that the death of our bodies is not the end, and that each person will exist forever.

When we have to make a choice between the Theory of Evolution and creation by God, it is important that we trust the teachings of the word of God! As we've seen throughout this book, even scientists keep finding evidence that the Theory of Evolution is wrong and the living things in our world could not have "just happened." How good it is to trust God's word and not the empty theories of human beings. How good it is to

know that you and I are special to God and that because of Jesus we can live forever with him.

Just For Fun

1 Do people just stop existing after their bodies die? What does the story that Jesus told about a rich man and a beggar suggest in Luke 16:19-31?

2 Find several pictures of your parents taken when they were your age. In what ways are you like them? In what ways are you different? In what ways, besides looks, are you like your parents?

3 What are you like? What are some of the ways you are different from other people you know?

4 What are some of the good choices you have made recently? What are some bad choices? How do you feel when you make a bad choice? A good one?

5 What important reasons can you find in this chapter to trust Jesus as your Savior and obey him?

THE BOOK THAT DIDN'T JUST HAPPEN

In the beginning was the Word, and the Word was with God, and the Word was God.

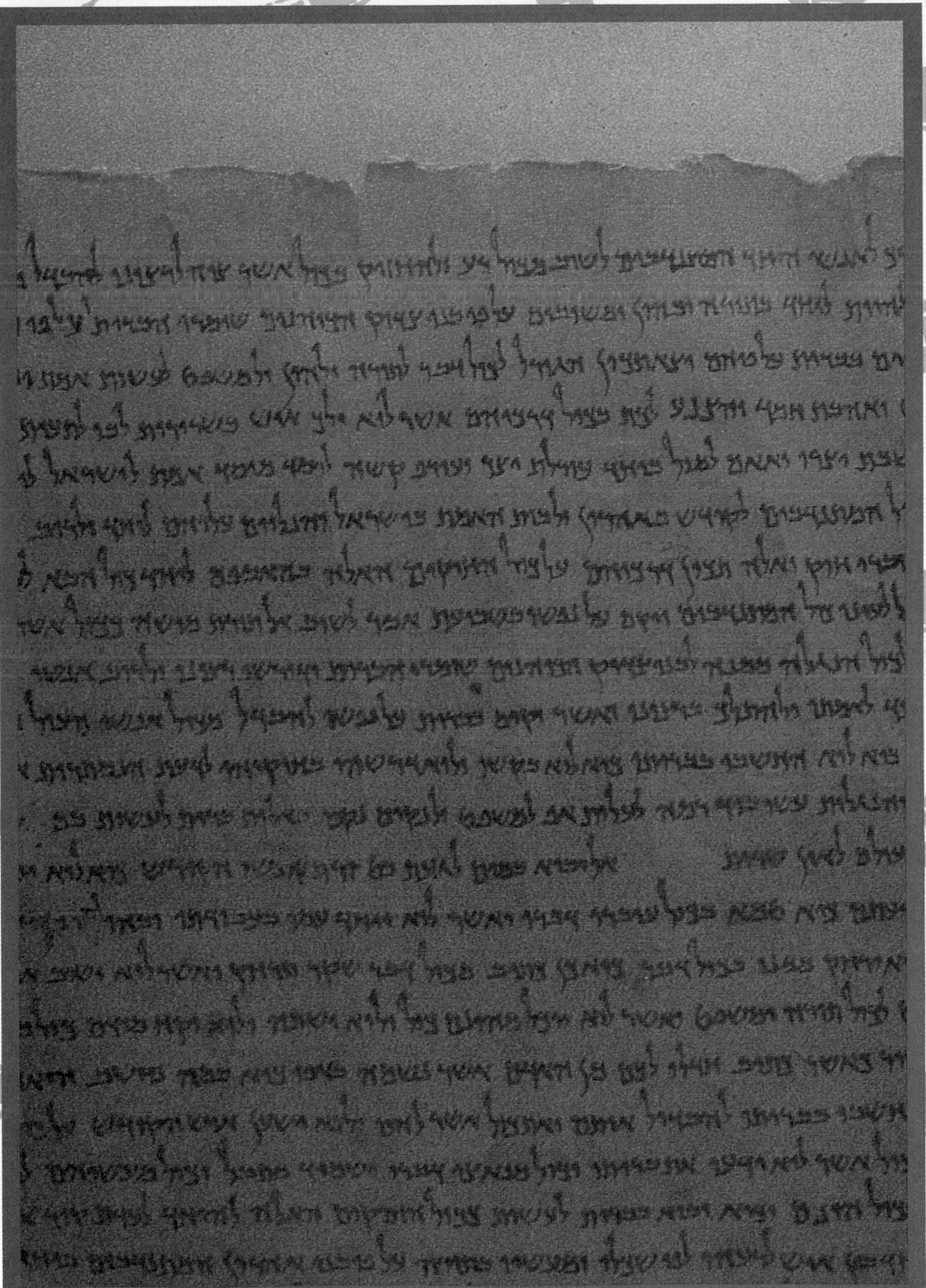

17 A SURE WORD

Many things in nature convince us that the Theory of Evolution ❓ is not a good explanation for origins. Creation is a far better explanation. And there is a book that tells us *how* God 📖 created everything: the Bible. When we study it, 🎯 we realize that the Bible, like our universe, could not have just happened without God! 💚

In this book we've examined two very different ideas about origins. One view is that everything just happened by chance. After a Big Bang billions of years ago started our universe, the matter which came from that unexplained explosion just happened to cool into stars. Our sun, one of those stars, just happened to have planets around it. One of these planets, Earth, just happened to be

Weaver birds tie complicated knots as they form their nests. Such complex patterns in nature are evidence of a Creator. But we need the Bible, a special revelation, to learn what the Creator is like.

the right distance from the sun and to have just the right mix of water and other elements. As Earth cooled, chemicals in an ancient sea just happened to come together in the right way, and these dead chemicals came alive. As ages passed, the first living cells just happened to take on plant and animal characteristics. As more ages passed these tiny cells just happened to cluster together to become larger living creatures. As even more time passed, living creatures just happened to become more and more complex. Somehow some living creatures just happened to turn into other living creatures—fish became amphibians and reptiles. Some of these just happened to turn into birds and mammals. And eventually one line of living creatures supposedly turned into human beings.

This view, called the Theory of Evolution, is thought of today as the "scientific" view of origins. Schoolbooks and many school teachers, as well as newspapers and magazines, often assume that the Theory of Evolution is a proven fact. Actually, there is more scientific evidence *against* the Theory of Evolution than there ever was *for* it. Conditions on Earth are too right to support life to have just happened. No non-living mix of chemicals has ever come alive, even though scientists have tried all sorts of ways to make it happen. In fact, we've seen that mathematical analysis indicates life could *never* begin from non-living chemicals.

No single-celled living creature has ever been known to turn into a many-celled creature. When scientists have tried to make living things mutate, they have never been able to make even a fruit fly turn into anything besides a fruit fly. The fossils on Earth do not support the idea of a gradual change from one kind of living creature to another. And no one can even guess how such a change might possibly have happened.

The idea that our universe, our Earth and living things "just happened," as the Theory of Evolution insists, simply is *not* supported by the discoveries of science itself!

The other view of the universe, of Earth and of life, is that each was created. Nothing "just happened." Instead, a living, powerful and intelligent Being planned and made all things. This view is supported first of all by the amazing design we see everywhere. The Earth is ideally designed to support life, and each complex living creature is designed for life on this planet.

In fact, the evidence against everything happening by chance is strong evidence that there *is* a Creator! Why? Because there are only two possible ways all that exists could have come to be. Either it all happened by chance (the Theory of Evolution), or it all happened on purpose (was created). So evidence against Evolution is evidence for creation!

This is why the Bible says in Romans that people have always known some things about God. The things God has made show that he must exist, because they simply could not have just happened! The Bible says that

> Since what may be known about God is plain to them, because God has made it plain to them. For since the creation of the world God's visible qualities—his eternal power and divine nature—have been clearly seen, being understood from what has been made, so that men are without excuse.
>
> For although they knew God, they neither glorified him as God nor gave thanks to him, but their thinking became futile and their foolish hearts were darkened.
>
> Romans 1:19-21

Knowing about God

The things that God has made, then, tell us that God must exist. For our universe, Earth and living creatures to exist, there simply *must* be a creator.

But there is much more that people need to know about God. The creation tells us that God is powerful and wise. But what is he really like? Why did he create the world? Why did he create people? Does he love us? How does God feel about us when we do something wrong? Will

God punish sin? Will God forgive people? What kind of persons does God want us to be? Can God help us be his kind of persons?

Christians are sure that God has answered those questions in the Bible, where he also tells us about himself as Creator. The Bible says very clearly that God created our universe, our Earth and living creatures. And the Bible describes a special act by which God created human beings. We Christians believe in creation partly because the evidence of science shows it is the best explanation for what exists. But we believe in creation mainly because we trust what the Bible tells us.

What's so special about the Bible?

The Bible is God's word to human beings. It is *revelation*. In the Bible we are told things about God and his actions that we could not discover in any other way. And the source of this revelation about God is God himself! Again and again the human writers of the Bible speak in God's name. "Here is what the Lord says," is found over 2,000 times in the Old Testament alone! There are other religions which teach the universe was created. But only in the Bible does the Creator speak to human beings.

In the Bible alone we read about *how* God created, simply speaking to bring the stars and Earth and animal life into existence. In the Bible alone we discover that human beings were made in God's image and likeness. In the Bible alone we find the explanation of why only humans can appreciate beauty, invent new things, and tell the difference between right and wrong. And only in the Bible do we learn about sin and about God's plan to bring us eternal life through Jesus Christ.

The Bible's claim to be revelation is important to us when we think about origins. That claim means that, while the Theory of Evolution was made up by mere human beings, what the Bible says has been communicated to us by God himself.

Some people view the Bible as nothing more than a human writing. They think that the Bible is merely a report of what different men have thought about God. If this is true, the Bible would contain only good religious ideas. And no one would have to respect the guesses of its writers about creation or even about sin and salvation.

But what if the Bible *is* revelation and everything the Bible teaches is true? Then its account of the creation of the universe and Earth and the special way human beings were formed in God's image, would be true!

The facts that science has discovered are strong evidence for creation. But if the Bible is God's word to human beings, the statements in the Bible about creation would be *proof*! So we need to ask, is there evidence that the Bible is the word of God and that what it says is true?

But what kinds of evidence should we look for to show that the Bible is God's word? Well, for one thing, the Bible would need to be historically accurate. God doesn't make mistakes. And, for another, there should be something about the Bible that is clearly supernatural.

The Bible's historical accuracy

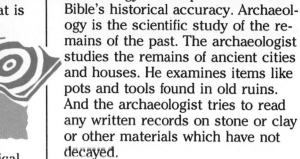

The Bible reports many historical events. Perhaps we can begin by asking if what the Bible says about history is accurate.

Many times in the past, people have attacked the accuracy of the Bible. At one time scholars said Moses could not have written the first five books of the Bible. In Moses' time, they argued, there was no written language!

Scholars also doubted the trustworthiness of Daniel. It couldn't have been written when it claims, they said. Daniel talks about events that took place long after the author was supposed to have written it. So, the critics said, the book of Daniel must have been written after those events took place. Besides, they said, the author was wrong about the names of rulers and other details of that time. Only a person who wrote much later would make such mistakes.

These, and many other charges, have been made to try to show that the Bible contains historical mistakes. Surely if the Bible were the word of God, it could not contain historical errors! If the Bible were true, it would not contain books written long after they claim to have been written, by people other than the supposed author. Let's look at some of these claims. The science of

archaeology has helped us test the Bible's historical accuracy. Archaeology is the scientific study of the remains of the past. The archaeologist studies the remains of ancient cities and houses. He examines items like pots and tools found in old ruins. And the archaeologist tries to read any written records on stone or clay or other materials which have not decayed.

Archaeologists have worked for many years in lands mentioned in the Bible. They have learned much about the places and people mentioned there. Nelson Glueck, a famous Jewish archaeologist, wrote that "no archaeological discovery has ever controverted [proved wrong] a bibilical reference." And he calls the Bible's history "incredibly accurate."

What about all those critics who thought that they found historical errors in the Bible? They have been proven wrong time after time. For instance, we now know that Moses *could* have written the first books of the Old Testament in any of several different well-developed written languages used in his time. Archaeological discoveries have shown that Daniel was right in naming the rulers of his time, and the critics were wrong. In fact, Daniel had information that a person writing hundreds of years later could not have had! Daniel wrote the book at the time he claims to have written it.

There is much, much more. Archaeological discoveries have shown that the customs of 2,000 years before Jesus fit the Bible's account of Abraham. The Genesis account of Joseph in Pharaoh's court

For thousands of years Bible books were carefully copied by hand and preserved because people believed they were the word of God.

uses just the right technical terms and refers to practices followed in Egypt's royal court 1,800 years before Jesus. Again and again archaeological finds have proved the accuracy of the Old and New Testament historical accounts.

No, historical accuracy does not prove that the Bible is the word of God. But historical accuracy is evidence that we can trust the Bible.

Can we prove the Bible's origin?

There is one fascinating thing about the Bible that is definite evidence of its supernatural origin. That is prophecy, telling about the future.

God says through the prophet Isaiah,

> I am God, and there is none like me.
> I make known the end from the beginning,
>   from ancient times, what is still to come.
> I say: My purpose will stand,
>   and I will do all that I please.
>   Isaiah 46:9b,10

If the Bible writers really did tell the future, this is strong evidence. Only God could know the future. Only God could tell the future. So if the Bible foretells the future, then it is God's Book, and its claim to be revelation is true!

What kind of things do the Bible writers prophesy? And have they happened? Here is a list of just a few Old Testament prophecies that have come true. There are many more like these. And there are also prophecies that have not yet come true because they are about Jesus' return.

Ezekiel, writing around 592-580 B.C., made a prediction about the city of Tyre. His prediction (in Ezekiel 26) was

Nebuchadnezzar will destroy the mainland city (26:8). Nebuchadnezzar of Babylon did this in 573 B.C.

Tyre will be made a bare rock, and the city's ruins will be thrown in the water (26:4,12). Alexander the Great did this. Alexander used the ruins of the mainland city to build a roadway to an island where the people of Tyre had retreated. This happened in 332 B.C., over 200 years after the prophecy.

Where the city once stood, fishermen will spread their nets, but the city will not be rebuilt (26:5,14).

Modern Tyre is not built where the old city stood. Even today, some 2,500 years after the prophecy, fishermen spread nets on that rocky shore.

The prophet Nahum, about 661 B.C., wrote about the destruction of Nineveh. His prophecies about this great city, the capital of the Assyrian empire, announced:

Nineveh will be destroyed in "an overwhelming flood" (Nahum 2:6). Rivers that fed a 150-foot wide moat protecting the city overflowed and washed away some of the wall. Then the enemy army could enter the city. This is reported in Babylonian records.

Nineveh will be totally destroyed (Nahum 3:15). In about 612 B.C., an enemy attacked the Assyrian army outside Nineveh. The city was so completely destroyed that its ruins were not even located until the last century!

Archaeologists study remains of past civilizations. The findings of archaeologists show that the Bible is historically accurate.

Similar prophecies were made about Babylon. This city, which covered 196 square miles and was 56 miles around, was guarded by outer walls 311 feet high. This is about the height of a modern thirty-story building! The wall was 87 feet wide. Eleven cars could have been parked side by side on it.

Babylon not only fell just as the prophets foretold, but Isaiah, writing over a hundred years before, even named the man who took it: Cyrus (see Isaiah 44:24-28).

When we look through the Old Testament we find many prophecies about places and people—and everything happened just as those who spoke God's word said it would.

But what about people today who claim to be able to tell the future? Each January some magazine will ask so-called psychics to guess what will happen in the new year. Now and then some of their guesses are right, but always others are wrong.

Bible prophecy is different. What the Bible says will happen *always* takes place. And Bible prophecies are usually about things that will happen hundreds of years after the person who made them has died. How, for instance, could Isaiah have "guessed" that the person who conquered Babylon would be named Cyrus?

How could Daniel guess the different nations that ruled for 400 years after he died? Yet Daniel told ahead of time about the Persians, the Greek conquerer Alexander and the four generals who divided up Alexander's empire when he died.

Some of the most amazing Bible

prophecies are about Jesus. We will look at a few of them in the next chapter. But you may already know that over 700 years before Jesus was born, Isaiah said the Savior would be born in Bethlehem. Isaiah also described Jesus' death, and other prophets told details about his life on Earth.

Now, none of these prophecies could "just happen." Mere human beings could not have guessed, hundreds and hundreds of years ahead of time, what would happen to cities and nations and individual people. But the Bible tells about the future, often.

Fulfilled prophecy is evidence that the Bible really is God's word. Only God can foretell the future. Since the Bible accurately foretells the future, we can trust it as God's word and know that what the Bible teaches is true.

How is archaeology related to prophecy? Some people have claimed that Bible prophecies were written *after* the events happened. For instance, they have said that the book of Daniel could not have been written some 530 years before Jesus because it tells so accurately what happened during those years. But archaeological discoveries have shown that the book of Daniel is accurate: it tells details about persons and customs in the royal court that would only have been known by someone who was there!

The historical accuracy of the

Many prophecies in the Bible give details about how ancient cities like Nineveh were later destroyed. The cities that were not rebuilt were eventually covered with dirt to form city-mounds called "tells" like the one shown above. The even slopes and flat summits make unexcavated tells different from natural hills.

Bible shows that the books of the Bible were written when they claim to have been written—*before*, not after, the things that were prophesied.

Yes, the Bible is a book that didn't just happen. It is a revelation from God. The Bible's account of creation, not the Theory of Evolution, is true.

Just For Fun

1 What is one important thing that sets God apart? Read about it in these Bible passages: Isaiah 41:21-24; 45:20-21; 46:8-11; 48:5-7.

2 See if your church library has a book on Bible archaeology. If it does, look up what it says about the book of Daniel.

3 Find out how an archaeologist works. What would be most interesting about being an archaeologist in Bible lands? What would be hardest?

4 Historical accuracy and fulfilled prophecy are both evidence that the Bible didn't just happen. Which do you think is the stronger evidence?

5 Explain to someone how Bible prophecy helps us be sure that what the Bible says about creation is true.

18 HOW WE KNOW WE CAN TRUST WHAT JESUS SAID

Bible prophecies about Jesus and the miracles that Jesus performed show that he truly was the Son of God. So what Jesus said about creation can be trusted. And Jesus taught that God, not Evolution, is the source of everything that exists.

After Moses led the people of Israel out of slavery in Egypt, they were given a warning. God's people were warned not to go to fortune-tellers or to astrologers for supernatural guidance. God promised that he would guide his people and send them prophets. God would speak through the prophets, not fortune-tellers.

But how could a person tell if someone who claimed to speak for God was really a prophet? What if a person was lying? God gave his people tests. A true prophet would be an Israelite. He would speak in the name of the Lord and would not disagree with what the Lord had said. And, what the prophet predicted about the future would happen (Deuteronomy 13:1-3; 18:17-22)! So accurately telling the future was proof that God spoke through a person

and was evidence that what he said could be trusted.

It's the same with the Bible. The fulfilled prophecies in the Bible show us that what the Bible says is really from God. We can trust the Bible. We can be sure it is God's word.

Prophecy about Jesus

Many prophecies in the Bible are about Jesus. These prophecies do more than show that the Bible is the word of God. They also show that Jesus, who fulfilled the prophecies, truly is the Son of God.

The Old Testament promised that God would send a leader to deliver his people. The promised leader

In Bible times how could people know who was a true prophet? One important test was that a true prophet could accurately tell the future.

would be someone that God appointed to save his people.

Long before Jesus was born, the Jewish people realized that many prophecies were about this leader. The New Testament shows us that Jesus Christ fulfilled those prophecies!

What are some of the prophecies, and how were they fulfilled? The chart on page 162 shows just a few of the prophecies that Jesus fulfilled in his birth, his life and in his death by crucifixion.

Actually there are many more prophecies about Jesus than are listed on the chart. What are some others? Here are more Old Testament verses with the New Testament record of their fulfillment.

Jesus was to be betrayed by a friend (Psalm 41:9; John 13:18; Matthew 10:4), who was paid thirty pieces of silver (Zechariah 11:12; Matthew 26:15). This money was to be thrown down in God's house and then used to buy the field of a potter (Zechariah 11:13; Matthew 27:5,7). Jesus was to be silent when falsely accused (Isaiah 53:7; Matthew 26:59-63; 27:12-19). Jesus was to be mistreated (Isaiah 53:3; Matthew 27:26), spit on (Isaiah 50:6; Matthew 26:67) and mocked (Psalm 22:7-8; Matthew 27:31). Dying, Jesus was to pray for his persecutors (Isaiah 53:12; Luke 23:34). People would gamble for his clothes (Psalm 22:18; John 19:23-24).

Long before Jesus was born these and other Old Testament passages were recognized as prophecy about the promised Messiah.

Then Jesus was born. And not just one or two of the Bible prophecies fit his birth, life and death. *All* the prophecies about his first coming fit perfectly!

How likely is it that a person could "just happen" to fulfill all these predictions so perfectly? In *Science Speaks*, Dr. Peter Stoner uses probability theory to test how likely it is that just eight of the many prophecies about Jesus could happen by chance. His results, checked by the American Scientific Affiliation, show that the chance any man might have lived from when the prophecy was made to the present time, and fulfilled all eight is just 1 in 100,000,000,000,000,000. Dr. Stoner illustrates by saying that if we took that number of silver dollars and spread them over Texas, they would

PROPHECIES ABOUT JESUS THAT HAVE COME TRUE

THE OLD TESTAMENT PROPHECY

THE NEW TESTAMENT FULFILLMENT

JESUS TO BE BORN OF A VIRGIN

The Lord himself will give you a sign: The virgin will be with child and will give birth to a son, and she will call him Immanuel. [NOTE: This name means "God is with us".] (Isaiah 7:14)

Mary was pledged to be married to Joseph, but before they came together, she was found to be with child through the Holy Spirit . . . . All this took place to fulfill what the Lord had said through the prophet. (Matthew 1: 18,22)

JESUS TO BE FROM DAVID'S ROYAL FAMILY

"The days are coming," declares the Lord,
  "when I will raise up to David a righteous Branch,
a King who will reign wisely
  and do what is just and right in the land." (Jeremiah 23:5)

"Jesus . . . the son of David" (Matthew 1:1; Mark 10:47-48; Luke 3:31; Luke 18:38-39; Acts 13:22-23; Revelation 22:16)

JESUS TO BE BORN IN BETHLEHEM

"But you, Bethlehem Ephrathah,
  though you are small among the clans of Judah,
out of you will come for me
  one who will be ruler over Israel,
whose origins are from of old,
  from ancient times." (Micah 5:2)

Jesus was born in Bethlehem in Judea. (Matthew 2:1; Luke 2:4-7; John 7:42)

JESUS TO PERFORM MIRACLES

your God will come. . . .

Then will the eyes of the blind be opened
  and the ears of the deaf unstopped.
Then will the lame leap like a deer,
  and the mute tongue shout for joy.
(Isaiah 35:4-6)

Jesus went through all the towns and villages, teaching in their synagogues, preaching the good news of the kingdom and healing every disease and sickness. (Matthew 9:35)

JESUS TO BE CRUCIFIED LIKE A CRIMINAL

because he poured out his life unto death,
  and was numbered with the transgressors.
For he bore the sin of many,
  and made intercession for the transgressors.
(Isaiah 53:12)

They crucified two robbers with him, one on his right and one on his left. (Matthew 27:38; Mark 15:27)

JESUS' SIDE TO BE STABBED

They will look on me, the one they have pierced. (Zechariah 12:10)

One of the soldiers pierced Jesus' side with a spear. (John 19:34) cover the whole state two feet deep! Dr. Stoner then explains:

Now mark one of these silver dollars and stir the whole mass thoroughly, all over the state. Blindfold a man and tell him that he can travel as far as he wishes, but he must pick up one silver dollar and say that this is the marked one. What chance would he have of getting the right one? Just the same chance that the prophets would have had of writing these eight prophecies and have them all come true in any one man, from their day to the present time, providing they wrote in their own wisdom.[1]

Bible prophecy about Jesus could not have "just happened" to be ful-filled. God *must* have spoken through the prophets. And Jesus *must* be the Son of God, as the Bible says he is.

Hundreds of years before Jesus was born in a manger in a cave like this one near Bethlehem, the prophet Micah foretold the town of his birth. Dozens of Old Testament prophecies give details about Jesus' birth, life and death.

The evidence of miracles

When Jesus lived on Earth, he did many miracles. These miracles showed the people who saw them that God was with Jesus. People could trust what Jesus said.

What is a miracle? The miracles that the Bible reports are simply things that everyone who saw them realized could not happen without an act of God.

Jesus' first miracle was done at a wedding. He turned water in twenty-gallon jars into wine (John 2:1-11).

Another time Jesus was sleeping in a boat in a terrible storm. When the boat was about to sink, Jesus' disci-ples woke him up. Jesus stood up and told the storm to stop. Immedi-ately the wind stopped, and the water was calm. Everyone knows that storms do not just happen to stop when a person tells them to (Mat-thew 8:23-27).

Many times Jesus healed incurable diseases. He made a man walk who had been an invalid for thirty-eight years (John 5:1-11). He gave sight to a man who had been born blind (John 9). Even modern medicine can't perform such healing. People with sicknesses like these do not just happen to get well. And they are not made well when some stranger tells them to be healed.

Jesus even called a man who had been dead and buried for four days back to life. The man's name was Lazarus, and he lived in the town of Bethany, near Jerusalem (John 11:1-44).

People who watched these miracles knew that what they saw could not just happen. What they saw was something supernatural, not something that was natural.

Were Jesus' miracles real?

Some people have suggested that Jesus didn't really perform miracles. They say that people in Bible times were ignorant and easily fooled. Or they say that people just made up the miracle stories later. But these objections are clearly wrong. In Jesus' day the Jewish homeland was even smaller than Israel is today. Jesus taught there and performed miracles for at least three years. Everyone would have a chance to see Jesus and his miracles for himself.

People then were not ignorant at all! They knew very well that a paralyzed man or a person born blind does not just happen to get well. They knew that a few pieces of bread and fish can't feed 5,000 people (Matthew 14:15-21). It was because they knew that what they saw was *not* natural that, the Bible says, they were amazed, stunned and even frightened.

The miracles Jesus performed were out in the open, in front of crowds of people who watched everything Jesus did. In that small country many people knew the sick persons Jesus healed. Many people had been to Lazarus' funeral and had seen his dead body. No, the people of Judah and of Galilee *knew* that the

miracles Jesus did were real.

But there is even more evidence. Jesus had enemies. These enemies hated Jesus and argued against his teaching. But even his enemies had to admit that Jesus did perform real miracles (John 3:2). The enemies of Jesus tried very hard to prove his miracles were nothing but tricks. When Jesus healed a blind man, these enemies "did not believe that he had been blind and could now see again." So they sent for the man's parents and questioned them. The parents answered, "We know he is our son, and know he was born blind" (John 9:18-23). Finally Jesus'

There are many illnesses modern medicine cannot cure. But when Jesus was on Earth, he made the blind see and even raised people from the dead.

READ ABOUT JESUS' MIRACLES

SOME MIRACLES OF HEALING

Of soldier's servant	Matt.	8:5-13
Of two blind men	Matt.	9:27-31
Of a daughter	Matt.	15:28
Of a leper	Mark	1:40-42
Of a bleeding woman	Mark	5:25-34
Of a deaf and dumb man	Mark	7:31-37
Of a blind man	Mark	8:22-26
Of Peter's mother-in-law	Luke	4:38-39
Of a withered hand	Luke	6:6-10
Of a crippled woman	Luke	13:11-17
Of ten lepers	Luke	17:11-19
Of nobleman's son	John	4:46-54
Of paralyzed man	John	5:1-11
Of man born blind	John	9:1-7

SOME MIRACLES SHOWING POWER OVER NATURE

Over storms	Matt.	8: 23-26
Over fish in the sea	Luke	5:1-11
Over bread	John	6:1-14
Over water	John	6:19

SOME MIRACLES SHOWING POWER OVER SATAN

Over an evil spirit	Matt.	9:32-33
Over a demon-caused illness	Mark	1: 23-26
Over a demon harming a boy	Luke	9:37-43

SOME MIRACLES SHOWING POWER OVER DEATH

Raising Jairus' daughter	Matt.	9:18-26
Raising a widow's son	Luke	7:11-15
Raising Lazarus in Bethany	John	11:1-44

enemies gave up trying to show that his miracles were faked. They knew that Jesus *did* perform miracles. So all they could do to fight against him was to say that perhaps he did miracles by Satan's power instead of God's power (Matthew 12:22-28).

When even Jesus' enemies admit that he does perform miracles, that is very strong evidence indeed.

So Jesus, the Son of God, showed that what he taught was true by performing real miracles that the people of his time knew were miracles. Miracles, like prophecy, are evidence that the Bible really is the word of God, and that Jesus Christ really is the Son of God.

We can believe what the Bible teaches. And we can be sure that what Jesus taught is true.

What did Jesus teach about beginnings?

The Theory of Evolution says that the universe, our Earth and life itself "just happened." But Jesus, the Son of God, *knows* how everything began. What did Jesus have to say about beginnings? Whatever he said, we can be sure that Jesus tells us what really happened.

What really happened is that God created our world. Jesus said directly, "God created the world" (Mark 13:19).

What really happened is that God himself made human beings. Jesus said that when God made the world, he "made them [human beings] male and female" (Matthew 19:4; Mark 10:6).

Jesus knew *and said* that everything the Old Testament teaches is surely true (see Matthew 5:17-19). So we have Jesus' own word for it. The Earth, human beings and "all things" were created by God (John 1:3).

The scientific evidence is against the Theory of Evolution, even though many scientists believe in Evolution. But we Christians are sure that creation explains where the universe, our Earth, animal life and human beings really came from. The Bible teaches creation. And Jesus, shown to be the Son of God by fulfilled prophecy and by the miracles he performed, taught creation, too.

Today juries hear witnesses and decide court cases. Thousands of people saw Jesus perform miracles, and even Jesus' enemies decided that his miracles were real.

Just For Fun

1 Do you think a person could *ever* find a marked silver dollar in a pile of silver dollars spread two feet thick across Texas? How much chance do you think there is of all the prophecies about Jesus just happening to be fulfilled?

2 Read Isaiah 53. How many different prophecies about Jesus can you find there that you know were fulfilled? Hint: read about the crucifixion in Matthew 26-28.

3 Read in the Bible about five of Jesus' miracles. How many people saw them take place? How did these people react? What chance do you think there is that Jesus fooled people about his miracles?

4 How many reasons can you think of why it is safer to believe the Bible about creation instead of accepting what even the best scientists think?

5 Here are some New Testament passages about creation. What does each tell you? John 1:1-10. Romans 1:18-20. Colossians 1:15-18. Hebrews 1:1-3.

19 WHAT THE BIBLE TEACHES ABOUT CREATION

The Bible does not answer many of our questions about Earth and its history. But the Bible is clear on one vital point: Creation, not chance, explains the origin of the universe and the existence of life on Earth.

How many choices are there?

Suppose someone were to ask you some hard questions. "Where did the universe come from?" "How did life begin, and how did all the different kinds of living creatures get here?"

These are very difficult questions, as we have seen. But the answer you give will be very simple. In fact, *there are only two possible answers you could give*!

One possible answer is, "Everything that is just happened." This is the answer evolutionists give. They think the universe began in a Big Bang (which no one can explain).

They think the stars in our universe, the Earth and other planets formed gradually. Then, as Earth cooled, they think living things just chanced to come from non-living chemicals. Next they imagine that over millions of years tiny, single cells just happened to grow into the many different and complicated plants and animals on Earth today. They cannot explain how any of this happened, and there is much scientific evidence against each of these notions. But this is what people who accept the Theory of Evolution must believe. And this is one of the two possible answers that a person might give if asked how everything began, and where living things came from.

The other possible answer is, "God created our universe. God shaped our Earth and created living creatures."

Everything we see in nature either developed by chance or came from the hand of a Creator.

These two are the only possible answers to questions about the origin of the universe and about the origin of life! We don't need the Bible to know this. Even without the Bible, we would know that only two explanations of the beginning are possible. One of these two explanations must be right.

In this book we've examined some things that evolutionists, who give the first of the two answers, believe happened. We have seen some of the many reasons why what they say "just happened" cannot be true. It is much more reasonable to believe that God created than to accept the "it just happened" Theory of Evolution.

So we really do not need the Bible to tell us that there is a God, or that God created the world and living creatures. The Book of Romans says that "everything that may be known

about God [from nature] has been made clear." People cannot see or touch God, but his power and all that makes him God have "since the creation of the world. . . . been clearly seen" (Rom. 1:19-20). People who examine the evidence with an open mind can and will discover that it points clearly to God as Creator.

What we learn about creation from the Bible

The things that God has made show us that he exists. But there are many things about God that can only be known by revelation. These are things that no one would know if God did not communicate them to us in the Bible. From what God has made, people should be able to tell that God exists. But only in the Bible can we find out *how* God created, as well as many other important things. What do we learn from the account of creation found in Genesis 1? Here are several important truths.

God always existed. God existed before the material universe. He created the stars from nothing, and he hung our world in space.

God is all-powerful. We are amazed today at the vast size of our universe and the awesome energy of its burning stars. The God who made all this is far more powerful than anything in his creation. According to Genesis, God had only to speak the word and all things sprang into existence. We cannot begin to imag-ine how great God is.

God is especially concerned about Earth. After flooding space with light, God carefully shaped Earth. He gave it the waters and air that make our planet unique, the only home for life that we know of. The creation of the stars later, on the fourth day, tells us that even though Earth seems insignificant, it is more important to God than the rest of the universe!

God created life. Living plants, fish and animals were all special acts of creation. They did not come into existence by chance at all. In each case, God spoke and his word formed the different kinds of living creatures. The Bible says that God "created every living thing that moves in the sea" as well as all land

THE THEORY OF EVOLUTION VS. GENESIS

ORIGIN	EVOLUTION	GENESIS
The Universe	It began in a "Big Bang" billions of years ago.	God spoke, and the heavens were created.
The Earth	It began as a red hot ball that cooled and by chance developed the conditions needed for life.	God created Earth and carefully shaped it as a home for living creatures.
Plant and animal life	Chemicals just happened to combine to make life.	God spoke, and life was created.
Different kinds of fish, birds, animals and plants	Tiny living cells somehow multiplied and changed to make varieties of creatures.	God created the basic kinds of plants and animals, which were able to reproduce the same kinds.
Human beings	People are complex animals who happened to evolve somehow from a different kind of animal millions of years ago.	God created the first man and woman in his image. Humans are different from the animals and are special to God.

and air creatures. And God gave each kind of life the power to reproduce, so that the Earth might be filled with living things.

God created human beings. Genesis 1 and 2 carefully describe the creation of human beings. One man and one woman were made by God, in a special way. God did not speak human beings into existence but carefully shaped Adam's body from elements found on Earth and then breathed a special "breath of life" into him. The Bible says God created human beings in his own image. And we have seen just how special this is.

So the Bible makes it very clear. What exists now did not "just happen." God actively created all things.

When did God create?

Genesis answers our basic questions about creation. It teaches us that God was involved in every important event that the Theory of Evolution explains by chance. God created the universe. He created Earth. He created the basic kinds of living creatures, not just original cells. And God created human beings in a separate, special creation. But there are other questions that the Bible does not answer.

One of these questions is, "*When did God create?*"

Several hundred years ago some Christians tried to calculate the date of creation from the ages reported in Genesis genealogy lists. These lists name people and their "sons." The lists tell how long the people named lived, and when the "sons" were born.

In the years 1650 to 1654, the Irish archbishop James Ussher wrote a book called *Annales Veteris et Nove Testamenti.* Working from the genealogy records in the Bible, he calculated the date of creation to be 4004 B.C. Since he was an important religious leader, Christians of his day accepted his calculations as accurate. That's why many Christians today believe the world is not very old.

But James Ussher and others who made such calculations overlooked something important. The genealogy lists kept by the Hebrew people do not list *every* ancestor. They often list only *important* ancestors. And the word "son" in genealogies simply means "descendant." The "son" might be a grandson or even a great-great-great-grandson! So there is really no way to calculate the date of creation from genealogy lists in the Bible.

Often evolutionists will write that Christians think the world was created in 4004 B.C. But that is not true at all. Today many people know more about Hebrew genealogies than Ussher did.

In fact, there is nothing in the Bible to suggest how long ago creation might have taken place! The Bible tells us that God did create. But the Bible does not state when.

Some Christians think that creation happened a very long time ago. Others think it took place as little as 10,000 years ago. But all Christians agree on one thing. God, not chance, explains the origin of all that is.

Did God create in consecutive 24-hour days?

Genesis tells us that creation took place in six days and that on the seventh day God rested (Genesis 1:1–2:4). When the events of each day have been reported, the Bible says "evening passed, and morning came." Because the Bible speaks of evening and morning, many Christians think "day" is used in its ordinary, 24-hour day sense.

There is of course no reason why God could not have created in six literal days. God surely could have shaped our Earth, spun the universe, and generated living creatures. Time places no limits on a God who can create by simply uttering a word.

But not all Christians think that the creation took place in a single week! At times in the Bible "day" is used to refer to long periods of time (see 2 Peter 3:8). Even in Genesis 1, there is no mention of a morning and evening for the seventh day. Many argue that that "day" has not ended even yet. So some Christians have suggested other ways to understand the seven days of creation.

The gap theory. One theory suggests that God used a 24-hour day to accomplish each of the tasks described in Genesis. But, this theory suggests, there may have been long ages *between* each creative day! This would mean, for instance, that God did shape and water our earth, making the seas and the dry lands on the second day. But then he waited a long time before creating plants.

Then, on another day, the third day of Genesis, God created plant life. But he may have waited millions of years while plants grew and developed over the whole earth.

The day-age theory. According to this theory, the "days" of Genesis 1 were not just 24-hours long. Instead the word "day" is to be understood in its meaning of "a long period of time." Christians who suggest this theory point out that if "day" does mean just a period of time, what Genesis teaches fits quite well with what most scientists think about the age of the Earth.

Today some people who are called "theistic evolutionists" hold this theory. The phrase "theistic evolutionist" means that a person believes in God (he is a *theist*), but that he also believes the Theory of Evolution. Such persons think that God created the world billions of years ago and then used Evolution as a tool to make it liveable. They also think that God created the first life but again used Evolution to shape the plants and animals that exist today. Some (but not all) theistic evolutionists even think that human beings evolved from animals, and then were given special spiritual life by God to make them different from their animal ancestors.

But the Bible is very clear that human beings were specially created by God. The Bible also makes it clear that the basic kinds of living creatures were directly created by God. The idea that God used Evolution as a tool is not a very good one and is not supported by scripture.

The revelatory-day theory. One other theory has been suggested by Christians. Perhaps the "days" in

Genesis were not really days of creation. Perhaps the seven were days in which God showed Moses what he had done!

This would mean that one day God showed Moses how he had divided light from darkness. The next day God showed Moses how he divided the waters and made the atmosphere of Earth. And the next day God showed Moses how he gathered the waters of Earth and made dry land appear. This theory suggests that the seven days were days in Moses' life, not days on which creation actually took place.

Each of these theories is a theory about how we should understand what Genesis is saying. A person can accept any of these interpretations of Genesis without denying God or rejecting the Bible. It is possible that one of these understandings of Genesis will turn out to be right. But since we do not know for sure, we should not be dogmatic about the one we prefer.

There are interpretations of Genesis that are clearly wrong. For instance, some say the Genesis story is just a "myth." They think it is a made-up story which expresses a true religious insight, but what Genesis describes did not really happen. No Bible writer treats Genesis as a made-up story, and Jesus himself talked about Adam and Eve as real people, directly created by God.

While Christians can disagree about whether the days of Genesis are 24-hour days, we cannot disagree about creation itself. The Bible does teach that God created. God made the universe. God made our world. God made living creatures. And he made human beings the most special of all.

The Genesis Flood

Evolution says that life began by chance. The Bible—and the evidence—says that God made all that exists. Here the Bible and evolutionist scientists are in direct conflict.

Many are convinced that there is another area of direct conflict between the Bible and currently accepted scientific theory.

Modern geologists and paleontologists know that their old idea of how Earth's surface was shaped is wrong. Geologists used to believe in *uniformitarianism*. This is the idea that all changes on Earth have taken place very slowly, using only forces like wind and rain and earthquakes that we experience today. Today most geologists admit that many features of Earth's crust must be explained by cataclysms. Scientists now accept the idea that Earth may have been struck by giant meteors and realize

Three mountains have a role in the dispute between people who believe in creation and evolutionists. Mount Sinai, shown here towering over the plain below, is where God revealed the creation account to Moses.

Mount Everest, the tallest mountain in the world, has rock strata at the top that were deposited by water. This mountain reminds us that our world has not always been as it is now.

that great areas of Earth have been scoured by massive, unexplained floods.

Some Christian scientists argue that the Flood described in Genesis 6–8 was just such a cataclysm. Some even believe that the Flood was so terrible it may have caused the continents to shift and form great mountain ranges. These scientists argue that the Genesis flood is a good explanation for many of the mysteries that geologists have been unable to explain.

All Christian scientists accept the Genesis flood as something that really happened. They accept the Bible's report that the Flood was sent as divine punishment and that it wiped out all human beings except Noah and his family. But they dis-

agree about just how the Flood affected Earth. Many do not believe the Flood was the kind of worldwide disaster that can explain many of the unusual features of Earth's crust. They think instead that the Flood was local, limited to a relatively small part of the globe.

What *does* Genesis say? Here are verses from Genesis 6–8 that describe the Flood.

So the Lord said, "I will wipe mankind whom I have created, from the face of the earth—men and animals, and creatures that move along the ground and birds of the air (6:7).

They rose greatly on the earth, and all the high mountains under the entire heavens were covered. The waters rose and covered the mountains to a depth of more than twenty feet. Every living thing that moved on the earth perished. . . . Everything on dry land that had the breath of life in its nostrils died. . . . The waters flooded the earth for a hundred and fifty days (7:19-24).

The water receded steadily from the earth. At the end of the hundred and fifty days, the water had gone down, and on the seventeenth day of the seventh month the ark came to rest on the mountains of Ararat (8:3-4).

Christians who think the Flood was local say this description is "phenomenological." That means the passage accurately describes how something *looked* to Noah. For instance, the Bible talks about the sun "rising." We know that the Earth is turning around, and that the sun is not actually rising. But *it looks as if* it is rising to a person on Earth. Everyone uses this same kind of language. Even our newspapers report that "sunrise will be at 6:05." So if the Bible is using this kind of expression in Genesis perhaps it means only that all the high areas that Noah could see from his home were covered by a terrible and long lasting flood. People who think the Flood was local also argue that while all humans were killed, probably mankind had not yet spread over very much of the Earth.

Christians who believe in a local flood may also use scientific arguments. For instance, there isn't enough water on and around planet Earth to cover all mountains to a depth of twenty feet. So, they say, the Flood *must* have been local.

What are arguments for a planet-wide flood? First, people who believe in a cataclysmic flood think the description in Genesis should be taken literally and not interpreted phenomenologically. The Bible says that "even the highest mountains were covered." When Noah's ark came to rest it was on one of the mountains of Ararat, which are high mountains in what is now Turkey. The Bible says all birds and animals on Earth died. Even if people had not spread out over the world, the creation account suggests that animals covered the Earth when they were created. Just reading the account in Genesis seems to imply a world-wide instead of a local flood.

But what about the scientific problems? People who believe in a worldwide flood answer that we need not assume mountains were as tall in Noah's day as they are now. After all, even evolutionists think that mountains were once, somehow, thrust up from much lower levels. There *is* enough water to cover our planet if the mountains were lower and the sea beds relatively higher.

So people who agree that at one time a flood did wipe out humankind, just as Genesis says, do not always agree about how widespread that flood was.

You and I should study and come to our own conclusion about which interpretation is best.

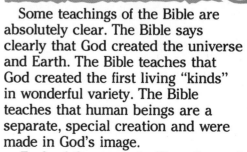

What we can and cannot know

Some teachings of the Bible are absolutely clear. The Bible says clearly that God created the universe and Earth. The Bible teaches that God created the first living "kinds" in wonderful variety. The Bible teaches that human beings are a separate, special creation and were made in God's image.

Each of these great affirmations of the Bible is actually supported by scientific evidence!

What the Bible does not say is just how long ago creation happened. There are even different ways to understand the seven "days" spoken of in Genesis. So we can't say for sure that we know how old Earth is or how long ago God made human beings.

The Bible also clearly teaches that there was a flood, sent by God as punishment for sin. This flood destroyed all living human beings except for Noah and his family. What we cannot say for sure is just how long ago the Flood happened. We also cannot say for sure how this flood affected the surface of our Earth. Even those who believe that the Flood was world-wide cannot know for sure which features of Earth's crust were caused by the Flood and which were caused by something else.

Should we Christians be concerned because there are some questions about creation and about Earth's past that we cannot answer? Not really. There are always limits to human knowledge.

We should be confident in our faith. We should trust the things that the Bible does clearly teach and not worry about the issues it does not deal with. And we should remember always, despite what we may hear or read, that the scientific evidence is *against* the Theory of Evolution and *for* creation, as creation is taught in the word of God.

Just For Fun

1 Read the creation account in Genesis 1. Write in the margin of your Bible the important things Genesis 1 teaches.

2 Do you think the days in Genesis 1 are seven 24-hour days? Why or why not?

3 Read the account of the Flood in Genesis 6-8. Do you think it was a world-wide flood or just a local flood? Why? Also, read 2 Peter 3:3-7. Did this Bible writer seem to think the Flood was local or world-wide?

4 Who do you know whose faith would be strengthened or whose questions would be answered by reading this book? Why not loan your copy to him or her or purchase another copy to give as a gift?

5 Explain in your own words why we should not be concerned about questions we cannot know the answers to.

20 ALIVE NOW AND FOREVERMORE

The Bible tells us ✝ where the universe and human beings came from. God, not Evolution, is the source of everything. And the Bible does more. It tells us the destiny of this universe and 🕊 of each individual person! We know how evolutionists and creationists view origins. But what does each view imply ❓ about the future?

It's something to think about. Just suppose for a minute that you believe the Theory of Evolution. You think that the universe, our Earth and all living creatures just happened. You think that human beings evolved from some other kind of animal millions of years ago.

If this is your belief about the past, then what do you believe about the future? Well, if you're like many who teach the Theory of Evolution, you probably think that the human race is going to get better and smarter. You may think people will develop spaceships and head out to visit the stars. You may expect people to find other planets like Earth and establish colonies. You might think that humans will find alien life. Someday—and you may get very excited about this—a more

Evolutionists often dream of an exciting future exploring the stars. But what would the future really hold if the Theory of Evolution were true?

highly evolved human race may even populate the universe!

But even though you expect millions and millions of years of exciting adventures ahead for humanity, there are two things that may make you sad. First, you feel sure that someday it all will end. Scientists tell you that the stars will finally die. A great darkness will come, and a terrible cold will grip the dead remains of the universe's hundred million galaxies.

Second, you won't be there to see any of it. You will be dead. You will never think again, never feel again, never love or have anyone love you. In a hundred years or so no one will even remember that you were once alive. So what difference will it make to you if whatever has evolved from human beings reaches the stars thousands of years from now? You won't be there. And no one will care. You will be dead. And no one will know that you ever lived.

What about you?

According to the Theory of Evolution, you have no future. You are just an intelligent animal, in a race of animals that developed by chance. Other animals die and are gone, and, so the Theory of Evolution teaches, you will die and be gone, too. Death is your destiny—and your end.

So if the Theory of Evolution is right, you have no hope for the future. You may live for 70 or 80 or even 102 years. But that's not long compared to the billions of years

evolutionists think the universe has existed. And then you will die, and that will be the end.

But suppose the Theory of Evolution is *wrong*. Suppose God created the universe and that human beings are special. If God is the explanation for *beginnings*, it's possible that he has a plan for the *end* as well!

If God created human beings, there may be hope! If people are important to God, perhaps death need not be the end for individuals!

Even a person *without* the Bible, who realizes that a universe so wonderfully designed must have a Creator, can find hope for the future in the existence of God.

But we *have* the Bible! In the Bible God tells us that each individual is so important that death cannot be the end. Each individual will be himself or herself forever.

So *you* have a future beyond the death of your body. The real you, the person who thinks and feels and loves, will keep on thinking and feeling forever and ever. For you, death will not be the end.

What does lie in the future?

In the last few chapters we've seen that the Bible is a book that didn't just happen. God, who created the universe, gave us the Bible through human writers who spoke and wrote his word. Archaeology shows us the Bible is historically accurate. Prophecy and miracles prove the Bible's supernatural origin. We know that we can trust the Bible and believe what it says.

So what does the Bible tell us about the future of the universe and about the future of individuals? Let's see what the Bible says lies ahead.

For this universe. One day God will act to end this universe and to destroy our Earth. The Bible says

The heavens will disappear with a roar; the elements will be destroyed by fire, and the earth and everything in it will be laid bare.... That day will bring about the destruction of the heavens by fire, and the elements will melt in the heat.
2 Peter 3:10-12

In the end God, who created this universe, will destroy it. So the universe had a definite beginning, and it will have a definite end.

A new creation coming. But the story does not end with the destruction of this universe. The Bible says God will create a new universe! In 2 Peter the Bible goes on, "But in keeping with his promises we are looking forward to a new heaven and a new earth, the home of righteousness" (2 Peter 3:13). The last book of the Bible talks about this new creation.

Then I saw a new heaven and a new earth, for the first heaven and the first earth had passed away, and there was no longer any sea. I saw the Holy City, the new Jerusalem, coming down out of heaven from God.... I heard a loud voice from the throne saying, "Now the dwelling of God is with men and he will live with them. They will be his people, and God himself will be with them and be their God. He will wipe every tear from their eyes. There will be no more death or mourning or crying or pain, for the old order of things has passed away."
Revelation 21:1-4

This description of a new creation where human beings will be with God and live forever is what most people mean when they talk about "heaven."

Heaven, and hell, too. Human beings are too important just to stop existing. Each of us will keep on thinking and knowing, and keep on being himself or herself, forever and ever.

The Bible tells us that God wants us to spend eternity with him. He wants us to be with him so much that God's Son became a human being and died to pay for each person's sin. Those who realize that Jesus is Lord, and who follow him as the Savior, can have their sins forgiven and can look forward to a joy-filled forever.

But many people choose to reject God. God reveals himself to everyone through what he created, but many people refuse to give glory to God or be thankful—and they keep on sinning (Romans 1:21). God offers complete forgiveness of sins through Jesus. But many ignore God's Son. They will not obey him as Savior and give up their sin.

God has done everything he can do to forgive human beings and bring them to heaven, but some people just refuse to turn to God.

The Bible tells us about the tragic future of these people, too. Revelation describes a "fiery lake of burning sulfur" where sinners are thrown (Revelation 21:8). And Jesus also talked about this fire of punishment (Matthew 5:22; Mark 9:43; Luke 16:23-24). So each individual will exist forever. Some will be with God. But some will be separated from God in a place of terrible punishment.

This may be the most important reason to argue against the Theory of Evolution. Evolution teaches that there is no need for God: everything can be explained without him. If God isn't needed, many people are not going to think about the future. If people just die and that is the end, why become Christians anyway?

But if God is, and people are not animals but are his creations, death is not the end. If we will exist forever and forever, it's important to live the way Jesus wants us to and to be sure about our personal relationship with God now!

Resurrection ahead

We've looked at some evidence that the Bible is God's word and did not just happen by chance. There is another important proof as well.

Resurrection isn't just something that will happen in the future. Resurrection has *already* happened. Jesus was raised from the dead!

In fact, the Bible says that Jesus was "declared with power to be the Son of God by his resurrection from the dead" (Romans 1:4). The resur-

rection was final proof that Jesus is God's Son. It is proof that God will raise you and me from the dead, too. But why are we so sure that Jesus was raised from the dead?

Actually we know more about the death and resurrection of Jesus than any event in history! There are eye witness accounts. There are writings by people of the time who tell of the resurrection, and often these people were not Christians. There is more indirect evidence too; there are things that happened that simply would not have happened if the resurrection weren't true.

What is some of the evidence that proves Jesus really was raised from the dead?

First, Jesus was really dead. Before Jesus was crucified, he was beaten terribly. Many people watched him die, including soldiers who knew death well. One soldier stuck a spear into Jesus' side to make sure he was really dead.

His body was taken down from the cross and wrapped in graveclothes. The people who did this knew he was dead, and they put him in a cave that had been carved into rock to make a tomb. A giant stone, so heavy it took several men to move it, was put in front of the opening of the tomb. This giant stone was sealed by the Roman officials, and a guard of soldiers was set to watch it. According to custom, at least four soldiers would be members of this guard. Everyone was sure that Jesus was dead, and the people who killed Jesus wanted to make sure that his body stayed in the tomb.

But why did the people who killed Jesus put a guard outside his tomb? We don't usually send soldiers to guard a dead person! The reason is that before Jesus was killed he had told people what would happen. He said that he would be killed. And he promised that he would come to life again! We can read those promises in the Bible in all of these places: Matthew 12:38-40; 16:21; 17:22-23; 20:18-19; 26:32; 27:63; Mark 9:10,31; 10:33-34; 14:28,58; Luke 9:22-27; John 2:19-22; 12:32-34; chapters 14–16.

Second, in spite of everything, the tomb was open and empty. Three days later there was an earthquake. The great stone was moved, and the soldiers became unconscious.

When people came to visit the tomb, it was empty! The cloths that had been wrapped around and around Jesus' body were still there. But Jesus' body was not in them. Several of the visitors saw an angel outside the tomb who told them that Jesus had risen from the dead and was gone.

If the tomb had not really been empty, then Jesus' enemies, who had had him killed, could have just taken people to the grave and said, "See, you don't want to believe in Jesus. Here is his body." But they did not

do that at all. The tomb really was empty, and there was no dead body for his enemies to show anyone.

The enemies of Jesus didn't want people to believe that he was raised from the dead as Jesus said he would be. After all, if Jesus was raised from the dead, his claim to be the Son of God would be proved! So his enemies lied. They said the disciples came and stole his body while the soldiers were asleep. And they bribed the soldiers to tell this lie, too. They also promised the soldiers to protect them if they lied.

Why would the soldiers need protection? Because soldiers who fell asleep while on guard would be punished by their officers. And the punishment for a Roman soldier falling asleep on guard was *death*!

Of course, the disciples had not come to steal Jesus' body. The disciples had been so frightened when Jesus was taken that they all ran away. They did not try to rescue Jesus when he was alive. Would they be brave enough to face soldiers just to steal his body once he was dead?

And, if the soldiers had been asleep, moving the heavy stone would have made enough noise to have awakened the soldiers.

So few in those days believed that Jesus' body had really been stolen. But everyone knew the grave was empty. The enemies of Jesus would not have tried to convince people the disciples took his body if the body were not gone!

Third, Jesus was seen alive by many witnesses! After Jesus was raised from the dead, many people saw him. Here is the list of people that the Bible gives.

Jesus was buried in a tomb similar to this one in Jerusalem. But Jesus was raised from the dead, just as those who follow him as the Savior will be.

PEOPLE WHO SAW JESUS AFTER HIS RESURRECTION

Mary Magdalene

John 20:14

Two Marys

Matthew 28:1f

Simon Peter

Luke 24:34

Two unnamed disciples

Luke 24:13f

Ten apostles, without Thomas

John 20:19f

Ten apostles, with Thomas

John 20:26f

Seven by a lake

John 21:1f

Over 500 at one time

1 Corinthians 15:6

Many at the ascension

Acts 1:9-10

All these people who saw Jesus alive knew him and could not have been fooled. It was really Jesus, not just someone who looked like him. Luke says that when he wrote his gospel he talked with many who were actual eyewitnesses (Luke 1:2). When Luke wrote the book of Acts, he added that after Jesus' death "he showed himself to these men and

gave many convincing proofs that he was alive" (Acts 1:3).

Fourth, the witnesses really believed that Jesus was alive. How do we know that the witnesses didn't lie?

Well, for one thing, the same disciples who were so afraid and ran away when Jesus was taken suddenly became brave! Acts tells us how Peter and John and the others faced the very people who had Jesus killed—and refused to obey them. Certainly they wouldn't have risked being killed too if they were not very sure that Jesus had risen from the dead.

Sometimes some people make money from religion. Did the followers of Jesus make money by starting a false religion? Not at all. Instead, most of them were persecuted and

A giant stone rolled in a track like this one to seal Jesus' tomb. It was moved that resurrection morning, and the tomb was empty.

suffered much for following Jesus. If they did not know that Jesus was raised from the dead, they would never have suffered so much to tell people about him.

Yet this is just what the followers of Jesus did. They told people about Jesus and called on people to accept him as Savior. And every time they preached, they announced gladly that God had raised Jesus from the dead.

Just listen to this bold sermon preached by Peter after he healed a cripple in Jesus' name. Peter did not preach this to the crowds, but to the very leaders who had Jesus killed!

> If we are being called to account today for an act of kindness shown to a cripple and are asked how he was healed, then you know this, you and all the people of Israel: It is by the name of Jesus Christ of Nazareth, whom you crucified but whom God raised from the dead, that this man stands before you healed.
>
> Acts 4:9-12

So Jesus really was raised from the dead. Jesus is alive today. And Jesus can save people like you and me from our sins.

You and I live in a society in which many people no longer think God is necessary. They think that everything that exists can be explained without God. They think that the Theory of Evolution describes how living things developed and explains the origin of human beings.

Jesus returned to heaven from the top of this mountain, watched by his apostles. Millions of people have believed in Jesus during the last 2000 years. We never need to be ashamed that we believe in a God who is both Creator and Savior.

In this book we've looked at some of the scientific evidence that Evolution (with a capital "E") did *not* happen. The evidence for creation is far stronger than the evidence for Evolution, even though schools and textbooks only tell one side of the story. I hope that this book helps you realize that you don't have to be ashamed of believing in creation or of trusting what the Bible says. It's really more reasonable to believe in creation and to believe the Bible, than to reject them.

But it is most important of all to realize that, because God specially created human beings, you are important to him. You are so important that he will never let you stop existing; even after death you will be able to think and feel. You will be yourself, forever and ever.

Because you will exist forever, it is so important to think about your future, now. How good to know that if you trust Jesus and choose to follow him you will be raised as Jesus was and forever live a joyful new life with God.

Just For Fun

1 Either God created the universe and life or everything happened by chance. How would you explain to someone why there are only these two possible explanations of how everything began?

2 Explain how an evolutionist's view of the past is related to his view of the future. How is a creationist's view of the past related to his view of the future?

3 What did you know about the Bible's teaching on the future before you read this chapter? What is new to you?

4 Look at chapters 18 and 19 and list five kinds of evidence that proves what the Bible teaches is true.

5 What do you think is the best reason of all for you to be a Christian and to choose to follow Jesus?

NOTES

Chapter 1. The Universe and Its Origin

   1. Nigel Henbest, *Mysteries of the Universe* (New York: Van Nostrand Reinhold Co., 1982), 181.

   2. Eric Barrett and David Fisher, eds., *Scientists Who Believe* (Chicago: Moody Press, 1984), 112.

Chapter 2. Dead Planets, Living World

   1. Jonathan Weiner, *Planet Earth* (New York: Bantam Books, 1987), 811.

   2. Weiner, *Planet Earth*, 811.

Chapter 3, The "Odd Planet"

   1. Weiner, *Planet Earth*, 74.

   2. James Lovelock, *Gaia: A New Look at Life on Earth* (Oxford, England: Oxford University Press, 1979), 71.

   3. Barrett and Fisher, *Scientists Who Believe*, 5.

Chapter 4. World in the Making

   1. Henry M. Morris, *What Is Creation Science?* (San Diego, Ca.: Master Books, 1982), 118.

   2. Weiner, *Planet Earth*, 203.

   3. Weiner, *Planet Earth*, 197.

Chapter 7. "Life" in a Test Tube

   1. Dr. Robert Jastrow, *Until the Sun Dies* (New York: W. W. Norton & Co., 1977), 62.

   2. J. Keosian, *The Origin of Life and Evolutionary Biochemistry* (New York: Plenum Press, 1974), 218.

   3. Dr. James F. Coppedge, *Evolution: Possible or Impossible?* (Grand Rapids, Mi.: Zondervan, 1973).

Chapter 8. The Mystery of the Moths

   1. Ruth Moore, ed., *Evolution* (New York: Time-Life Books, 1969), 113.

   2. Lane P. Lester and Raymond G. Bohlin, *The Natural Limits to Biological Change* (Grand Rapids, Mi.: Zondervan, 1984), 89.

   3. Lester and Bohlin, *Natural Limits*, 88.

Chapter 9. The Record in the Rocks

   1. Stephen J. Gould, *The Panda's Thumb* (New York: W. W. Norton & Co., 1980), 181-82.

   2. Stephen D. Schafersman, "Fossils, Stratigraphy, and Evolution," in *Scientists Confront Creationism*, ed. by Laurie R. Godfrey (New York: W. W. Norton & Co., 1984), 234.

   3. Darwin, *Origin of the Species*, 217.

   4. John Phillips, *Life on Earth: Its Origin and Succession*, 1860 reprint (Salem, NH: Ayer Co. Publishers, 1980), 18.

Chapter 10. The Same, Yet Different

   1. Moore, *Evolution*, 112.

   2. Morris, *What Is Creation Science?*, 24.

Chapter 12. More Wonders of Design

   1. Morris, *What Is Creation Science?*, 22.

Chapter 13. When It Takes Two

   1. Nevil D. Buffaloe, *Animal and Plant Parasites* (Englewood Cliffs, NJ: Prentice Hall, 1968), 32.

Chapter 18. How We Know We Can Trust What Jesus Said

   1. Dr. Peter Stoner, *Science Speaks* (Chicago: Moody Press, 1968), 107.

INDEX
It Couldn't Just Happen

187

Dr. Lawrence O. Richards is a leader in children's education. He has written over 100 books, including the *International Children's Bible Handbook,* the *Believer's Promise Book, The Expository Dictionary of Bible Words,* the *Word Bible Handbook* and the *Answers for Youth* series for kids.

Richards has also written several textbooks including *A Theology of Children's Ministry* and *Creative Bible Teaching.* His textbooks are used in most Protestant seminaries and Christian colleges in the U.S. and have been translated into 17 foreign languages.

Richards is a graduate of the University of Michigan and Dallas Theological Seminary. He holds a doctorate in social psychology at Northwestern University. He has taught both at the Graduate School of Theology of Wheaton College and at Princeton.